WHO & ME

The memoir of
Doctor Who producer

Barry Letts

1925 – 2009

fantom publishing

First published in this form 2009 by Fantom Films
fantomfilms.co.uk

A catalogue record for this book is available from the British Library.

Standard Paperback Edition ISBN: 978-1-906263-44-7
Hardback Edition ISBN: 978-1-906263-43-0

Typeset by Phil Reynolds Media Services, Leamington Spa
Printed by MPG Biddles Limited, King's Lynn

Front cover photo © TopFoto
Rear cover photo © BBC Worldwide Limited (*Radio Times* Magazine)

Portions of this book have previously been released by BBC Audiobooks Ltd.

CONTENTS

FOREWORD

What can I say about Barry Letts? Well, to begin with, we've been working colleagues and friends, best friends, for 40 years. We met in 1969 when Barry took over as the new producer of *Doctor Who*. It's no exaggeration to say that his arrival saved my job, and probably the show as well.

I'd been on *Who* for a year as a sort of assistant trainee script editor. The show was flagging, the script situation was in chaos, and I had no real authority to sort things out. Then the previous producer and script editor left to set up another show, Barry took over and things began to change.

I always used to say, half-jokingly, that about this time four very important things happened on *Who* as a result of which the once-failing show became a roaring success. The show went into colour; Jon Pertwee became the Third Doctor; Barry Letts became producer; and I became full script editor.

'Modesty forbids my saying,' I used to go on, 'which was the most important...'

In fact, of course, it was the incredibly fortunate combination of all four. But if any one does predominate, it was undoubtedly the arrival of Barry as producer.

The producer is the show. People often ask what a producer does. The answer is – everything. He doesn't have any one job; his job is to oversee and facilitate everyone else's. He has, or had in those days, total control.

Barry had the first qualification for being a producer: he didn't want the job. A producer has so much power that people who want it shouldn't be allowed to have it – like the seekers of immortality in *The Five Doctors*. Barry's first love was directing. In fact he insisted on a clause in his producer contract that he was to be allowed to direct the occasional show, and he seized the opportunity to direct a *Doctor Who* serial whenever possible.

Over the next five years we became good friends and close working colleagues. I can say colleagues because of the generosity of Barry's nature. Although always the boss, he treated me as a friend and equal.

He never said 'I've decided...' but 'We've decided...'

During those years we turned the show around. We sorted out the script situation, evolving a collaborative method of working with writers, that resulted in better scripts arriving in time. Ratings rose and, for a few golden years, *Doctor Who* was one of the BBC's top shows.

It all came to an end when Jon, probably wisely, decided that five years was long enough. Barry was keen to get back to directing, and I went with the flow. It was the end of an era.

What can I say about Barry himself?

The American comedian Will Rogers once said, 'I never met a man I didn't like.' Well, I never met a man who didn't like Barry Letts.

He is kind, modest, sensitive, caring and charming. Since I'm none of these things, it's a wonder we got on so well. But we did – and we do!

This book will tell you about his time as an actor and director before *Who*.

Above all, it tells about his time as producer of *Doctor Who*.

I only hope you enjoy reading about it as much as I did sharing it!

Terrance Dicks
September 2009

INTRODUCTION

'I'm so glad you both could come,' said Russell T Davies to Terrance Dicks and me. 'Ever since we got together, Phil and I have been meaning to ask you to come and have lunch with us, but events just took over. We want you to know that we think your era was the best of the old *Who*...'

Over 35 years after we left *Doctor Who,* Terrance and I had been invited down to Cardiff for the première screening of the regenerated series. Terrance was script editor when I was producer. There was a reception beforehand, packed with press, but also with a lot of well-known faces to be glimpsed through the crowd.

Before we could even manoeuvre ourselves into the scrum around the wine bottles, Russell T Davies pushed his way through to us, with the producer, Phil Collinson.

And he went on to tell us that they were quite consciously trying to take what we had done and express it in modern-day terms. This first episode made it very clear, picking up the first Jon Pertwee story about the Autons. The intention was to give a signal to the fans that this was their own *Doctor Who,* brought up to date but keeping the spirit of the show at its best. And they've succeeded magnificently.

Of course, there've been some big changes – the biggest being the personalities at the centre. All the first eight Doctors and most of their companions 'talked posh', after all. At first, it was quite a shock to hear Chris

Eccleston's northern accent. But it's bang-on right. When *Who* started in 1963, the BBC was middle class to its core, and thought of its target audience as middle class. But *Doctor Who* is for everybody, and the new producers have recognised the fact.

But quite apart from that, it doesn't matter how much the Doctor changes his surface personality. On the contrary, one of its strengths has been precisely that each Doctor was very different from his predecessors.

I was very aware of that when I was producer. Jon Pertwee's dignified dandyish persona had been chosen as a contrast to the clownish 'space hobo' that Patrick Troughton had given us. And after I'd cast Tom Baker to take over from Jon, Philip Hinchcliffe, the incoming producer, and I invited him to have lunch with us at the Balzac restaurant (and a very good lunch it was) to meet Bob Holmes, the script editor, and to work out with the three of us his approach to the new characterisation.

The one thing we were all agreed on was that the last thing we wanted was a 'poor man's Jon Pertwee'; and what emerged, as a deliberate contrast, was the wild bohemian fourth Doctor, with his floppy hat and long scarf (though we didn't plan it to be quite so long!).

But the core Doctor is always the same – and remains the same in Chris Eccleston's and David Tennant's sparkling characterisations: eager for every new experience, and seizing upon each opportunity to fight against those, whether human or alien, who will use evil means to gain their own self-centred ends.

Thank you Russell, thank you Phil, thank you everybody.

I never appeared in *Doctor Who* when I was an actor. But having spent over 20 years living in the same world that Patrick Troughton, Jon Pertwee and, later, Tom Baker came from, I could talk to them in their own language.

The world we came from was a world where every town of any size had a repertory company, with a different play every week; where actors would happily take to the road in year-long tours; where the flickering, often distorted black and white images of television were only beginning to infiltrate the homes and minds of the Great British Public, as we sometimes called the amorphous multi-eyed creature we courted and on whose favour we depended.

So I had shared their hopes and their fears; and I knew that behind the public face of each of them there lived a very different and slightly odd being whose nerve endings were much nearer the surface than most.

When Chummy, my wife, and I were still 'in the profession' we had to make a conscious effort to stop referring to those outside it as 'real people'. Yet that's how different we felt. So in this book I've tried to give you some idea of the Patrick and Jon that I knew, what they were really like. Tom I'll have to leave until next time.

But it isn't just a book of gossip. I've also tried to let you know what it was like to be part of this extraordinary enterprise as it took hold of the public imagination and put down the roots which have allowed it to grow and flourish for over 40 years – and for how much longer? It's not strictly chronological; but not 'stream of consciousness' either; maybe halfway in between. Conversational perhaps.

I've chosen the title quite deliberately. This is a book about *Doctor Who*, certainly, but it's also a book about me. There'd be no point in writing it otherwise, considering all the excellent books which have already been published giving so much of the background of the show.

(Thank you, David Howe, Mark Stammers, Stephen James Walker, Peter Haining, Jean-Marc Lofficier. Time and again

you came to my rescue with precisely the detail I was searching for.)

What was my background? What was it like to be an actor in live television? How did I come to be a director, and then the producer of *Who*? And what was it like to do the job?

I've been honest with you. If I think I screwed up I say so. But if I'm proud of something, I haven't hidden behind the false self-deprecation that's customary.

What else? Well, I'm quite sure that amongst my readers there'll be those who are already involved in making television, or films – and many who would like to be. So whenever it seemed to fit, I've given you some tips on the best way of going about it, the kind of thing I'd have found invaluable myself.

And then there's Zen…

CHAPTER 1

When I first worked with Patrick Troughton in a TV studio, I was wearing a ridiculous wig.

You can't help being self-centred if you're an actor. After all, this self – this intensely intimate thing you've lived with all your life – is your stock-in-trade.

Many people think that actors in general, and stars in particular, have exaggerated self-esteem, that they are terminally conceited, even arrogant. Some may be. They certainly give that impression. But my experience (and I've been working with actors for more than three-quarters of my life) is that most are covering up an extreme vulnerability, that they are desperate for approval – and, yes, love in its broadest sense.

Like Jon Pertwee, for instance. But more of that later.

Certainly, when I first met Patrick Troughton in the scruffy church hall that was the rehearsal room for *Gunpowder Guy,* the half-hour play for children about Guy Fawkes which was to be my television debut, my actor's ego was still smarting from the wig-fitting I'd just had.

In 1605 the fashion for men was to have their hair hanging down each side of the face in a type of long bob, a style which was profoundly unflattering for practically anybody. As for me, I looked a proper onion; and so did the majority of my co-conspirators, as I saw when we got to the studio on the day of the performance – especially with those silly hats on.

But not Patrick as Guy Fawkes. With the clout of an established leading man, he'd been able to insist on an entirely inauthentic sweep of the side hair behind his ears, which gave him the look of a romantic hero.

Patrick was one of the early TV stars, particularly in children's television. He loved screen acting, both for television and in films. Kenneth More, with whom I worked in *Scott of the Antarctic* and *Reach for the Sky* (now come on, you're bound to get a bit of name-dropping in this sort of book), told me that he found theatre work boring, having to repeat your performance night after night. Patrick felt the same. He called theatre acting 'shouting in the evenings'.

The result was that Patrick was quite at home in the television studio, even so early in its development. For this was in 1950, well over half a century ago.

I'm what the historians call a primary source. I was there.

The picture was of course in black and white, and of very low definition (405 lines, for those with technical minds). ITV didn't come along until 1955, and BBC2 wasn't even being discussed as a possibility; so there was only the one channel – and it was live. And that made quite a difference to the actors, believe me.

It couldn't be anything else but live. Even telerecording – the filming of the picture as it was being transmitted – wasn't yet practical. The problem of electronic video-recording certainly hadn't yet been solved. The difficulty of transferring the well-established techniques of audio-taping to the visual medium was due to the enormous amount of information that would be needed to recreate each frame; and there were 25 (yes, 25, not 24 as in film) frames to every second.

The BBC's first attempt, a tape recorder which was really nothing but a very large version of an audio machine, had been demonstrated by Richard Dimbleby on *Panorama,* live. It had reels of one-inch tape about two feet in diameter, spinning so fast that if the tape broke, which was exceedingly likely, the whole reelful was likely to end up a tangled mess on the floor. It wasn't until the brilliant invention of the helical-scan machines, which slowed the tape to a manageable speed, that we could pre-record a show.

So all drama was live, apart from a minimal amount of pre-filmed location footage, which of course had to be played in as part of the transmission.

Like most actors I suffered from intense 'first night nerves', even though I'd learnt over seven years of theatre and radio experience to transmute the resulting adrenalin buzz into a heightened intensity of performance. But with *Gunpowder Guy*...!

We'd had one week's outside rehearsal, and a short day with the cameras in Studio D at Lime Grove, the former Gainsborough film studio; and now, at five o'clock on Guy Fawkes Day 1950, our performance was going to be watched by an audience of hundreds of thousands, if not a couple of million.

Not only that, but as we waited, fiddle-string taut, for the drop of the hand from Mike, the floor manager, that would cue us to leap into action, we gradually became aware that the wait was becoming agonisingly long.

At last, he gently let his arm drop. 'Relax everybody,' he said. 'The transmitter at Ally Pally has broken down.'

So we took a deep breath and relaxed.

Ten seconds later, his arm shot up again. 'Stand by!' he barked.

We stiffened into our characters, like a bunch of Madame Tussaud's waxworks.

Minutes ticked by.

'It's gone again,' said Mike. 'No, no! Stand by!'

This happened twice more, by which time I was ready to relinquish my television career forever.

I wasn't the only television virgin that day. As well as me, at least two more of us had been cast by Rex Tucker from the stable of actors he'd worked with when he was producing and directing drama for the Home Service, as Radio 4 was called then. And what's more, *Gunpowder Guy* was also Rex's first go at his new job.

I'd been used to Rex coming out of the control gallery in the radio studio in Leeds, smiling and saying 'Well done' to everybody even if there had been the odd minor cock-up during a live transmission (like my saying '...fuck-funking it' in a production of *Hobson's Choice*).

But on 5 November 1950 he came down the iron steps from the gallery as pale and shaking as the rest of us. 'Well, I suppose that was all right,' he said, obviously trying to forget the lost camera, the occasional prompt, the wrong position that had ruined the carefully constructed group shot, and so on and so on, just as we were.

And it *was* all right. Because none of this had fazed Patrick Troughton in the slightest. He'd given his usual strong performance, carrying the play as the character had to. Rex's boss, Cecil Madden, the new head of Children's Television, was very pleased with the show – and Audience Research later confirmed what a success it had been with the viewers.

It was a great lesson for the future: it's the director's job to tell the story, using all the means at his disposal – the cameras, the sets, the music and so on – but it's the writing and the acting that really matter.

'See you in the club,' said Patrick to us all, and in an undertone to me as he turned to leave the studio, 'I'm dying for a cigarette...'

He and I had already struck up an immediate friendship based on the fact that we were both heavy smokers. During the camera rehearsal in Studio D, whenever there was one of the tedious waits while they sorted out some technical problem, we would slip out onto the fire escape for a quick draw.

Though it took some five years of abortive attempts, I managed to give up – on 10 March 1962, just as the Royal Society of Physicians published the first unarguable evidence that smoking could, and most likely would, either give you lung cancer or kill you with a heart attack. It gave me just the extra boost that I needed and this time I made it.

Pat wasn't so lucky. Some years later he had to have a lung removed.

And then, in 1978, when he heard that I was about to produce Dickens's *The Old Curiosity Shop,* he got in touch with me and asked if he could play the villain, Quilp, as he'd played it for BBC television about 15 years before, and felt that he hadn't got it quite right.

I was delighted to agree of course, and so was the director, Julian Amyes; and when we came to the pre-filming on location our decision was proved to be right over and over again. This was going to be the definitive Quilp for our time.

However, if you were to view *The Old Curiosity Shop* now (it went out in the States on PBS as part of the *Once Upon a Classic* strand), you might spot that though it's Patrick in all the filmed sequences, in the studio interiors, recorded on video, the part is played, excellently, by Trevor Peacock. (They were enough alike for us to be able to save the large cost of remounting the filming).

Pat had had a heart attack after the exterior filming had been completed.

It was another heart attack that killed him in 1987, three days after his 67th birthday, and in America for a *Doctor Who* convention.

The trouble was… no, I'd better rephrase that. The fact that he threw himself into whatever he was doing with 110 per cent glee wasn't a trouble. It was intrinsic to his personality.

If you asked him to do something over and above the call of duty, he'd think for a moment, and then either say, 'No!' with absolute finality, or he'd say, 'Great! Great!' And give you far more than you'd asked for.

An example. One of the early jobs I had after I left acting in 1965 was to direct *The Enemy of the World*, the *Doctor Who* story in which Patrick played not only the Doctor but also the villain, Salamander, a look-alike who might have been his twin.

When the TARDIS first arrives in the Australia of the future in which the tale is set, it lands on a beach. The script called for the Doctor to pull off his shoes and go for a paddle in the sea. But of course the sea in question wasn't the semi-tropical warm bath of the Southern Hemisphere, but the near freezing English Channel near Littlehampton. So I asked him well in advance if he was happy to have a go.

A fairly long pause. Then: 'Great! Great! Tell you what, why don't I strip off to my long johns and go for a swim?' And that's just what he did.

That was Patrick Troughton.

I worked as an actor with Pat quite a number of times, and got to know him well, so when I was asked to direct *The Enemy of the World*, I was delighted that I would have the chance of working with him wearing a different hat.

It was the cherry on the delicious cake of being offered a proper six-part serial, after several months (which I'd thoroughly enjoyed) of directing twice-weeklies. I felt that I'd graduated, and was about to join the grown-up world.

Being grown-up is all very well; but it means you're exposed to all the vicissitudes that go with it.

As you can imagine, the most important element in the run-up to the production of a play, a film, or a television serial like *Doctor Who* is the script. Until the final version is available it's just about impossible to get on with casting, design, location hunting, scheduling… To an extent you can manage with storylines which tell you the content of each episode. But things do change. Or have to be changed.

When I arrived to start work on *The Enemy of the World,* I was presented with only a draft script of the first episode and just rough synopses of the rest.

I don't know whose fault it was. Innes Lloyd had been the producer for over a year, with his script editor, Peter Bryant, sometimes taking over from him for the odd story. Peter was about to take over completely, so his successor, Derrick Sherwin, was also on the scene.

The writer was the *Doctor Who* veteran David Whitaker, one of the pioneers who was the first story editor, and also wrote the third serial ever in 1963.

From what I learnt later when I took over as producer, it wasn't likely that he was responsible for the indefensible position I was put in.

Did I mention location hunting? The Australian beach wasn't the empty one you may remember if you saw it all those years ago. The lone script started with the TARDIS, containing the Doctor (Patrick Troughton), Jamie (Frazer Hines) and Victoria (Debbie Watling), appearing on the seafront of a crowded resort.

Apart from the cost, by the time we would be shooting summer would be well and truly over, so there would be no hope of using Southend or Margate as a stand-in for Oz.

The first decision was obvious: to change the word 'crowded', as in 'crowded beach', to 'deserted'.

But that meant, of course, that the attacks on the Doctor in the amusement arcades, the gift shops and the fast-food joints would have to be replaced by something else.

At least I was able to have an input into the story.

I can't remember whether I made the discovery of a certain news item or whether my production manager, Martin Lisemore, did.

The news story was about a hovercraft which had been built as an experiment by a retired Naval Architect who lived in Worthing on the South Coast – and he was delighted when we asked if the thugs who were trying to assassinate the Doctor could use it on the empty beach that Martin had found a few miles down the road. This was a pretty recent invention, a completely new concept: a vehicle/boat riding on a cushion of air over land and sea alike. The first giant to rival the cross-Channel ferries had gone into service about a year before – but ours was less than 20 feet long. It had a cabin capable of holding three people at an uncomfortable pinch.

Few people had seen one at all, so it was ideal for a story which was set a few years in the future.

But how were the Doctor and his companions to escape? The hovercraft could follow them just about anywhere...

Aha! They could be rescued by our guest star, Mary Peach, flying a helicopter. A super way... (super? There's a lip-smacking period word; well, we were shooting this in 1967, weren't we?) ...a super way to introduce the heroine of the tale, Astrid, a direct pinch from the leather-clad superwomen played by Diana Rigg and Honor Blackman in *The Avengers.*

But having introduced the helicopter, we'd have to get rid of it. It could be an embarrassment if Astrid could swoop in at any moment in the six episodes and sort things out like a hi-tech guardian angel.

And what about the thugs? We didn't need them any more, either.

An extract from the script (we and the gang have just seen the thugs steal the helicopter and take off):

```
ASTRID: Oh no! I told you we'd made it just
in time. There's a bad petrol leak. It'll
blow up!

AND IT DOES.
```

A clunky device, but it did the trick.

Martin found a film clip of a helicopter exploding in mid-air. It was one of the alternative shots of a model of the SPECTRE helicopter in the James Bond film, *From Russia with Love,* and Martin also managed to find a real one for us to use that more or less matched.

It worked so well that I later wrote the same thing into the black-magic myth, *The Daemons,* the first Jon Pertwee story that Bob Sloman and I wrote together. A sub-villain, chasing the Doctor and Jo Grant in the UNIT helicopter, flies into the 'heat-barrier' that Azal, the resurrected Daemon, has created over the village of Devil's End, and…

We used the same shot.

CHAPTER 2

Talking of James Bond and the helicopter...

As we'd got it on location for a day, I was determined to make full use of it. We got ahead of the schedule, and I had an idea.

In a film I'd seen fairly recently, there was a spectacular shot, obviously using a helicopter, which I thought we might duplicate; or rather, have a go at a poor man's version.

For more than 35 years, I've been convinced that the shot was in a James Bond film (probably *From Russia with Love)* but I've checked all those in existence in 1967, and I can't find it. Perhaps somebody can enlighten me.

Two people are having lunch together in a railway dining car. The scene finishes with a wide two-shot, a double profile, with one on each side of the table. They talk for a while, and then the camera pulls back, and we see that we have been looking through the window of the train.

But that's not all. The camera goes on pulling back, and up, and up, and up, higher and higher, until we can see all the carriages. And still it goes up, settling at last on a view of the entire train snaking its way through a miniature countryside.

'They'd have had a special mounting – probably gyroscopic,' said Fred Hamilton, our cameraman, when we broke for lunch and I said I wanted to try a similar shot in the afternoon, swooping up into the air from a close shot of the chief thug, played by Rhys McConnochie, firing at us.

Oh well.

But towards the end of the break, he sought me out where I was checking the positions of the afternoon set-ups, and said, 'I've had a word with the pilot, and we reckon we could have a go.'

The helicopter was one of those small jobs with a bubble cabin at the front. The pilot, whose name was Jack, had agreed to take the doors off, so that Fred, the mad glorious fool, could sit on the edge of the deck, with his feet on the right-hand skid, and do a hand-held shot. He was loosely attached with a rope, but that was more of a gesture to allay the anxieties of poor Martin, who was responsible for the safety of the unit, than a real safeguard.

There was a snag.

'I'll have to have somebody sitting on the other side of me, to balance Fred,' said Jack.

Ah.

Remembering the General Montgomery/Laurence Olivier principle… (what's that? Simple. You never ask anybody to do anything you're not prepared to do yourself) …I volunteered.

Admittedly I was strapped in, but the open space where the left-hand door had been was only a foot away. And normally even looking over the Clifton Suspension Bridge gives me the heebie-jeebies in my loins.

It wasn't a sound shot, of course, so we could dispense with the clapper board.

Start the engine.

Turn over.

'Running,' says Fred.

I signal to Martin. 'Action,' he yells, over the noise of the rotors. Rhys runs into position and starts firing his automatic. I touch Jack's shoulder, the signal for him to take off.

Up we go, with a heavy list to starboard. Well, Fred is a big lad, six foot two and counting, and I'm a measly five eight.

Now what? Down we come, settling back into the starting position.

'Do you mind if we have another go?' shouts Jack.

This time we swoop up, and up, and up, exactly as planned.

'Do you know,' said Jack casually after we'd landed. 'The three of us were as near being killed then as we're ever likely to be. Another couple of seconds and we'd have side-slipped into the ground, with Fred underneath...'

The shot worked beautifully.

At that time the number of *Doctor Who* half-hour episodes in a year averaged 40; indeed, in Patrick's last season there were 44. There was the short break in the summer, but apart from that the pressure on the actors and the production teams was relentless.

Having rehearsed from Monday to Friday in an outside rehearsal room – usually a church hall, or a youth club – they would find themselves, all too soon, with a full day's camera rehearsal in the studio on the Saturday, leading up to an hour and a quarter of recording in the evening.

Sundays were nominally off, but of course there were next week's lines to learn. It never let up.

So how did we fit in the location filming?

The rule of thumb was to have a day's shoot – up to six minutes of screen time – for each episode. So with a six-episode serial like *Enemy of the World* we had about a week to get everything in. But how could we, when our good Doctor and the other principal actors were back in London recording the previous story?

Doubles, that's how. In long shot. And then, at the end of the week, Pat, Debbie and Frazer gave up their precious Sunday to come down to Littlehampton to fill in all the closer shots.

The script position was so dire that the dialogue rewrites hadn't arrived by the time we went off to the coast; so we were in the position of improvising our lines to fit the situation. We all had a go.

THE HELICOPTER LANDS. THE PILOT JUMPS OUT AND SHOUTS TO THEM.

ASTRID: Quick! Over here!

THE DOCTOR LEAPS INTO ACTION.

DOCTOR: Come on!

VICTORIA AND JAMIE ARE TERRIFIED.

[Well, they would be, wouldn't they? Victoria's from the 19th century and Jamie from the 18th...]

VICTORIA: What is it?

DOCTOR: It's a chopper! A whirly-bird!

JAMIE: He says it's a bird...

DOCTOR: Come on!!

Additional dialogue by Patrick Troughton.

I had a nasty shock some weeks earlier than this when I was on my personal recce on the beach, all by myself, finding the camera positions.

The beach, which was a private one owned by the Littlehampton golf club, whose course was just the other side of the sand dunes, was deserted.

Not quite. In the distance a small figure was approaching from the direction of the lane almost a mile away, which was the main access. He waved to me, so I went to meet him. It was nearly ten minutes before I was close enough to see that it was a diminutive boy scout (in the khaki uniform of the day).

'Are you Barry Letts?' he said. 'Your secretary wants you to give her a ring. It's urgent.'

Of all the odd moments of my life, this must rank as one of the most surreal.

He'd found a note pinned to the gate – left there by the owner of the hovercraft!

'The bookers [*the contract department*] have been on to me,' said Rosemary. 'We've lost Mary Peach.'

Oh no! Innes had the policy of having a guest 'name' or two, in this case Bill Kerr and Mary. During the last few years, she had caught the public eye with a series of cracking performances for ITV, notably for *Armchair Theatre*. Her costume was already being made and we were due to start filming in just over a week.

It seemed that our booker had looked up the last fee that the BBC had paid her, when she was an unknown playing a relatively tiny part, and told her agent that this was the fee this time too. Non-negotiable.

The agent, quite rightly, said that in that case the Beeb would have to do without his valuable client.

And neither would budge.

This is just the sort of thing that a producer is there to cope with. But both Innes and Peter were away on legitimate *Who* business, sorting out a tricky location for a future story.

I spoke to the booker. And his boss. Would they listen to me? BBC policy, they said.

It took the intervention of the lofty Head of the Drama Serials Department to move them. And they still insisted on putting the final agreed amount into Mary's contract in scarlet ink, marked *SPECIAL FEE*, so that they could try the same trick again next time.

I'd sold the part of Astrid to Mary on the strength of the story synopsis, as there were no scripts to show her, and emphasising the *Avengers* connection. After all, hadn't playing the original turned Diana Rigg into a big national star?

And then episode five arrived from David, and Astrid wasn't even in it.

It had to be completely rewritten.

At a policy meeting of producers and script editors, attended by Terrance (I wasn't there) somewhat later than this, a lengthy discussion sprang up about scripts. Over and over again it was emphasised that late scripts were the bane of production.

And then a gloomy voice came from the back of the room. 'That's all very well – but when they do arrive, are they any bloody good?'

By the time *The Enemy of the World* had arrived on the screens of the millions panting with anticipation, it was a right old mish-mash of good and bad. It's a great pity that the only episode that survived, and was included in the video *The Troughton Years*, was one of the poorest. The stuff in the kitchen, for instance, goes on far too long. It's full of padding; and padding shows up at its dullest in a half-hour show.

And isn't it ridiculous that the VIP prisoner, Denes (played by George Pravda), is held in a corridor, rather than in a room?

The whole episode (number three) is lacking in tension. Nobody is in any real danger, except poor old Denes, and we don't know him well enough to care very much.

That's not to say that other episodes weren't a lot more exciting; the rewritten number five, for instance, where we visited Salamander's control caverns deep underground.

It isn't a typical *Who* story by any means. The central idea is that the villain Salamander fortuitously looks like the Doctor's identical twin, so that Patrick played both parts, and had the obligatory scene at the end when he meets himself. It was enough in the future for Salamander to be able to control natural events (via 'solar energy'. Eh?), such as volcanic eruptions and earthquakes, and using them to try to get ultimate control of the whole world. A James Bondish story.

As always, the whole thing is saved by Pat. His Salamander isn't the usual moustache-twirling melodramatic villain usual at that period of the programme, but a more than real monster of evil who chills the blood.

You're either an actor or you aren't. If you're not, you can spend years at an all-singing, all-dancing, copper-bottomed, organic drama school, and you'll still not fool those who know.

A good school can be invaluable in cutting and polishing a rough diamond, but if you're the real thing, you'll quickly learn on the job. Patrick went to a drama school, true, but neither of his two sons, David and Michael, did. Both stepped straight into the profession from school, and quickly made their mark.

David made his first professional appearance in a *Doctor Who*. But it wasn't as the young king in *The Curse of Peladon*, as some of you may think. Nor, as the real experts will know, was it in the first episode of *The War Games.* It was in *The Enemy of the World.*

David was on holiday from his last year at school. He'd already made up his mind that he was going to follow his dad, so Patrick asked me if I could give him a walk-on part, just for the experience.

He played the guard who got Jamie's elbow in his midriff – and collapsed so convincingly that I had to keep the camera off him so that the viewer wouldn't be distracted from the escape attempt.

As I'd expected, I enjoyed working with Pat, even though his view of the dialogue (whether by the author, the script editor or even by P Troughton Esquire) was not even a rough blueprint, but more an idea scribbled on the back of an old envelope. Speech as written:

DOCTOR: Ah, Mr Bloggs. Do come in. Take a seat.

Speech in rehearsal:

DOCTOR: Come in, come in. Mr Bloggs, isn't it? Do sit down.

Speech on the take:

DOCTOR: Oh, there you are. Come in and take a pew. Now then, Mr Bloggs...

This sort of semi-improvisation infuriated Jon Pertwee during rehearsals of *The Three Doctors:*

[Patrick finishes speaking.]

LONG PAUSE

JON: Is that what you're going to say?

PATRICK: Never mind what I'm going to say. You concentrate on what you're going to say.

JON: (PLAINTIVELY AND WITH BARELY SUPPRESSED IRRITATION) How can I know what I'm going to say until I know what you're going to say?

In the end they became good friends, appearing together at an American convention – in a playlet written by Terrance overnight in his hotel bedroom – which capitalised on their supposed antagonism, enjoying it so much that they insisted on two repeat performances.

We could have mounted a nationwide search with full press coverage and couldn't have ended up with two more different personalities than Jon and Patrick. They shared two things (and you could say the same about 'my' other Doctor, Tom Baker): when they were on the screen you couldn't take your eyes off them; and they were enormously likeable. Yet…

Jon: Over-sensitive; self-centred; worried (in spite of his very successful career); manipulative; a good 'performance' actor; indeed he was usually giving a performance even when he was just being Jon.

Pat: Quietly confident in spite of the inevitable actor's vulnerability I spoke of earlier (he hated to be teased); sure of his own worth; wouldn't suffer fools; a true character actor who transformed himself.

I was fond of them both.

Having worked with Pat so many times, I knew him as the good-hearted soul that he was. Jon was a kind and unselfish man as well; indeed, his sensitivity was extended to everyone else. He did a lot to turn our casts and crew into a cohesive and happy company. For example, when a newcomer (even playing a small part) arrived in the rehearsal room, he'd wander over and introduce himself.

'Hello, I'm Jon Pertwee. I play the Doctor.'

No, really?

He made good friends of all the stunt men and other actors who were regularly cast. He was amusing and charming, and could surprise you with flashes of unexected humility.

I'll give you an example.

The producer (which was my prime role by the time I was working with Jon) didn't go to the day-by-day rehearsals. So it came as a surprise, about halfway through his reign as the Doctor, when Sue Hedden, one of our well-established assistant floor managers, told me that the other actors were complaining about Jon.

Since the death of live drama, prompters were no longer necessary during the performance, but AFMs still 'carried the book' at rehearsal. It appeared that Jon wasn't making any attempt to learn his lines at home, but using the rehearsal time to get them into his head, much to everybody's annoyance.

I could see how this had happened. He was a very busy man. He was still keeping up the odd cabaret appearance; and since becoming a national star he was in constant demand for opening supermarkets and such (for a handsome fee) and charity bazaars (for nothing). Fitting in what actors call 'study' was just about impossible.

Luckily this was the last story of the season, and Jon had asked me if it would be possible for me to lay on a showing of a serial he'd missed on transmission. (This was of course long before the introduction of home video-recording.)

So I took the opportunity, when we were alone in the little viewing theatre after we'd seen the playback, to bring this up.

'You've been an actor, Barry,' he said. 'You know how difficult it is to learn your lines at home.'

'Yes,' I answered. 'But I also know that unless you make the effort, it just wastes time. It's really frustrating for the other actors – and the director for that matter.'

He didn't respond – and we repaired to the BBC club and drank a friendly glass of wine.

Now, it so happened that Sue Hedden was the AFM on the next story after the break, and when on the second day it came to Jon's first scene, he sailed through without a pause. 'Good God,' said Sue, 'You know it!'

'Yes,' said our star, in front of the entire company, 'Barry took me into a corner and gave me a bollocking.'

CHAPTER 3

But of course, 17 years had separated *Gunpowder Guy* and *The Enemy of the World*. How was it that I had moved from playing a smallish part in the one to being the director of the other? For that matter, where had I come from? How did the Fates steer me along the way that would lead me to being the producer of *Doctor Who?*

'We think we can turn you into a film star!'

How would you react if somebody said that to you? Especially if that somebody was speaking in the name of the famous Ealing Studios?

It was Robert Hamer, later to become famous as the director of such films as *It Always Rains on Sunday* and *Kind Hearts and Coronets.*

I was 18; it was Saturday 14 August 1943. No, I don't keep a diary; I remember the date because it was two days away from my going into the Navy. I'd just spent something like four months playing Taff, the apprentice deck officer, in *San Demetrio, London,* the true story of a bunch of British seamen who reboarded their abandoned oil-tanker, put out the fires and filled in the shell-holes, and brought her safely back home.

Robert Hamer was the Associate Producer, and had directed us for a while when Charles Frend fell ill.

They gave me £100 a year retainer for the three years I was in the Royal Navy – not to be spurned, especially in my first months as an Ordinary Seaman, a rating somewhat lower than the ship's cat.

And when I came out in 1946, I became a film star.

Well, no. As a matter of fact I didn't, as you may have noticed.

I had a three-year contract: £1000 for the first year; £2000 for the second; and £3000 for the third. Riches beyond the dreams of avarice, as Oswald Bastable says in E Nesbit's book *The Treasure Seekers.* The most I'd earned in my three years of weekly rep (yes, I became an actor at 15. The theatres were desperate. Nearly all the juveniles were busy fighting the war) was £6 a week – roughly £300 a year. Now I was on course to earn ten times that.

And what's more, I was going to become a star.

What went wrong?

While I'd been away, the sparky little Ealing Studios had been completely overshadowed by the Colossus of the Rank Organisation. My contract had been handed over to Rank. Instead of being one of half a dozen contract artists, I was one of 40. I was lost in the crowd.

But I wasn't really film star material. I'm a good actor, but I'm simply not good at selling myself. You have to play the game. I used to watch the others – Christopher Lee, for example – happily laying out their wares to the producers and the casting directors who came to the weekly 'cocktail party' laid on by the organisation for this very purpose: for them to meet the contract artists.

I was jealous, yes, but I knew I couldn't do it myself.

There were two long-term consequences of my two years with Rank. (Yes, only two years. They dropped me, and I don't blame them.) One, a colossal tax bill that took another two years to pay off; and two, meeting a girl, Muriel Pears, known as Chummy, who was playing a member of the cycling club in *A Boy, a Girl and a Bike,* the last film I appeared in under my contract. She was 18 years old, she had chestnut hair and freckles, and she was the most alive person I'd ever met.

Reader, I married her; and it was one of the best things I've ever done.

Before the war, if you were under 16, you could get into the cinemas in Leicester for sixpence, provided you bought your ticket before four o'clock.

In 1939, when I was 14, I went to see *The Wizard of Oz*, getting to the cinema at ten o'clock in the morning, and sat through three complete programmes: the main feature (three times); a B film (three times); the news (three times); a travelogue designed to empty the theatre (three times); and that wretched organist, whose rise from whatever circle of hell he inhabited between times was my signal to go to the gents and come back to a different seat, so that the ushers wouldn't spot me. I left the cinema at ten o'clock at night, starving, but purring inside. And all for sixpence.

At the Wyggeston grammar school we had a half-holiday on Wednesdays – going to school on Saturday mornings instead – during which the house rugby matches were played. Dick Attenborough (not Dickie in those days) and I were both in our house teams, so we would forgo the delights of an after-game shower, and shoot off as fast as our muddy legs would carry us to catch a tram ride into town – only a ha'penny if you were at school – to get to the cinema box-office before four o'clock. It was a narrow squeak sometimes but we always made it.

It was on the way home from one of these jaunts (walking to save the ha'penny) that we solemnly decided that if Tyrone Power could make it as a film star with that nose, the same shape that we shared, then we could too.

Dick did. I didn't.

Dick's Dad was the principal of University College, Leicester, which eventually became Leicester University. Coming from that world, he wasn't sure that his son's ambition to go into the theatre was an entirely good idea; and when Dick was 14 or 15, he was persuaded that Doctor sounded better than Actor (you could always be an amateur), and managed to persuade me too, at least to the extent of taking biology for a year, though I quickly reverted to my long-held ambition.

In those days, the equivalent of GCSE was the School Certificate. It was a very similar exam, with one crucial difference: it wasn't modular. You couldn't take your subjects separately. All had to be passed in one go or you were told that you'd failed. What's more, certain subjects were compulsory – English and Maths, for example. If you 'failed' in the summer, you were allowed to take the whole exam again in the winter term.

Dick flunked one subject (Latin, I believe) on the first occasion; and another on the second.

Perhaps he did it on purpose, because he was then allowed to apply to RADA (the Royal Academy of Dramatic Art) and won a scholarship, which didn't surprise me at all.

Dick has always had the knack of making instant friends with everybody, whether it was the local greengrocer or a famous film director. Quite apart from his undoubted dramatic talent, this, together with his incredible determination (think of the film of *Gandhi*; he remortgaged his house to get it off the ground), is the thing that has taken him to the very top.

Until I met Chummy, and learnt from her how to 'be myself' with anybody, I found it almost impossible: a great handicap when what you are trying to sell is yourself.

I didn't become a star. But I wasn't unsuccessful.

After more rep, and a nasty year which included a stint on night work at Wall's ice cream factory in Acton, a career I wouldn't recommend to anyone, I attended a mass audition for the second lead, the villainous Petty Officer, in the Number One tour (magic words to an actor) of the smash hit *Seagulls over Sorrento,* which had Ronnie Shiner as the star. It was 1953, and the part I was going for had been played for the four years of the London run by William Hartnell, who ten years later was to become the first Doctor.

I got the part, and my life was turned round.

After a tour of more than a year which was like a paid holiday (more trouble from a greedy Inland Revenue), back in London I landed the lead in the BBC children's Christmas special on Boxing Day 1954 – Prince Ahmed in *The Three Princes,* by Rex Tucker, directed by Shaun Sutton.

We had a day's camera rehearsal on Christmas Day (cold turkey reheated in the oven when I got home), another on the 26th, and did the show live in the evening.

When I left Lime Grove after the transmission – at this point the Television Centre was in the middle of being built – I could have jumped over the moon, like a striker who'd just won the World Cup with a last-minute penalty. A bit laboured as a simile maybe, but it expresses what was going on inside. At last I felt like a star.

The Three Princes launched me into a new career. For over ten years, albeit precariously, I managed to feed Chummy and myself, and the three children as they came along, by playing all sorts of roles both for the BBC and for all the commercial companies when they arrived. The majority of the parts were in children's television and most were worth playing, either leads or good supporting roles.

Those days of live television stand out in my memory as some of the best. Once you'd got used to it, the buzz of performance, of being able to inhabit a character, knowing that every little thought would come across without the need for projection (Patrick's 'shouting in the evenings'), was even better than playing in the theatre.

No, I must qualify that. If anybody ever asked me which I preferred, theatre or television, I used to say, 'Which do you prefer, roast chicken or chocolate mousse?'

I missed the intimacy of connecting to a live audience, certainly; it was one of the things that had brought me into the theatre in the first place. But live television was… well, different.

Perhaps it was the constant awareness that things could go disastrously wrong which kept the adrenalin high. And of course old hands regaled us with tales of legendary disaster.

The time, for instance, when Robert Speight, playing Thomas à Becket in *Murder in the Cathedral*, was waiting in precisely the circumstances in which we'd found ourselves with *Gunpowder Guy*. Suddenly, without any warning, the floor manager waved a frantic cueing arm at him. Speight thought it was a send-up, a joke, and responded with the two-fingered salute which means '…and up yours too, mate', only to see the camera's red light come on.

Without a pause he managed to guide his hand into a smooth blessing, making the sign of the cross: 'In the name of the Father, and of the Son…'

Or when the watching millions saw the dead King Lear, thinking he was off camera as rehearsed, clambering to his feet to be hoisted onto the attendants' shoulders for the exit of his regal corpse.

I had my own moments, of course. Playing the villain, Sir Daniel, in *The Black Arrow*, I had to give my henchman his sinister orders while I was eating my dinner. At the dress rehearsal, I was faced with an empty trencher.

'What sort of food will I be eating?' I asked.

'Dunno,' came the reply. 'The canteen's sending something down for the transmission.'

Fish and chips? Raspberry jelly?

But no, somebody had done their homework. Come the evening, I was confronted by a pile of chicken drumsticks. Very mediaeval.

Chatting away villainously, I picked one up. Tasty. But what to do with the bone?

Aha! Charles Laughton playing Henry the Eighth in a 1930s film had tossed the carcass he'd been gnawing over his shoulder.

So, over my shoulder went the drumstick; and, as it went, out of the corner of my eye I saw half my moustache go with it.

I finished the scene with my hand hiding my bald lip, and as soon as it finished was urgently scrabbling in the straw to find it. It was stuck back just in time for my next scene.

But, yes, I loved them, those live days.

Indeed, I was very disappointed when I was told one day that my performance as Lord Nelson was to be pre-telerecorded on film.

Until the take.

Turning arrogantly to leave an altercation with the fuddy-duddy Board of Admiralty, I strode to the door, tripped over my sword and fell flat on my face.

In a stroke I was converted into a fervent disciple of recording.

Live television? You could keep it.

CHAPTER 4

I became part of Shaun Sutton's so-called 'rep' – the band of actors he used over and over again, which included Colin Douglas (who became well-known as the grandfather in *A Family at War)*, Joss Ackland, Paul Whitsun-Jones, Pat Troughton, Nigel Arkwright, John Woodnutt and Roger Delgado, who later created the part of the Master in *Who*.

In *The Queen's Champion*, which Shaun also wrote, I was the traitorous Sir Thomas Wycherly, doing my best to assassinate Queen Elizabeth the First. Roger Delgado, in a nice twist as a loyal Spaniard, Don Jose, not only foiled the plot, but – in a duel fought in the sea – stuck his rapier through me.

My beautiful suede thigh-boots, especially hand-made by the best theatrical shoemaker in London, were ruined by the salt water. The costume designer was not pleased.

One year I was in 18 episodes of Shaun's serials.

But...

Oh Gawd. Bloody money. I'm not all that good with it even now. But then...

You see, there are very few actors, no matter how successful, who don't have bad patches when the work dries up. If you've got any sense, you cater for that and budget accordingly.

I didn't. The result was that I ended up with a perpetual overdraft, and an ever-present fear that the next bill to arrive would be simply unpayable.

But to face the facts (for instance, in working out the Income Tax figures as a freelance) would screw me up inside so badly that I had to walk briskly round the block before I could even sit down at my desk. It was much easier to put things off, have another glass of wine, and join Mr Micawber in hoping that something would turn up.

My inability to cope with the pounds, shillings and pence was one of the multiple symptoms of my worst fault: procrastination, especially concerning tasks of some consequence.

When I was a midshipman in the Royal Navy – navigating officer of a Coastal Forces craft patrolling for U-boats off the South Coast – the torrent of chart corrections so overwhelmed me that I would literally (and I mean that literally) beat my head against the wall of the chart house to take away the mental pain.

It was partly fear of course. Fear that I should miss something and put us on the rocks. In the event, the only time it could have happened was because I'd got something right. A light in the blackout proved to be an RAF beacon five miles inland, but my skipper decided that it was the next buoy in the swept channel (cleared of mines, that is) that we were following.

I managed to convince him otherwise, thank God. If I hadn't we could have crashed into the Dorset cliffs, but I was scared out of my wits in case I was wrong, that I'd missed an Admiralty Fleet Order which had a vital change.

Putting things off nearly put paid to my marriage; and it was this that eventually put me on the path which led me into the clear.

What was that path?

Maybe *Planet of the Spiders* – which takes place in a Buddhist meditation centre – could give you a clue.

But back in 1965 something had to be done about our parlous financial situation. Although I was playing leading parts, I was very far from becoming a 'star'. It was becoming increasingly obvious that I would probably stay in the second rank for the rest of my time as an actor.

It wasn't the first time I'd had these thoughts. Right at the beginning of my new screen career, I'd played the Indian Gentleman in *Sara Crewe* – or was it called *The Little Princess?* No matter. I was talking to Peggy Livesey, who was playing the Head of the school, about the difficulty of climbing the professional ladder.

'Even if you make it,' she said, 'you can still find yourself in trouble. Look at my brother.'

Her brother? Roger Livesey, one of the big film stars of the 1940s. Think of *The Life and Death of Colonel Blimp; I Know Where I'm Going;* and *A Matter of Life and Death.*

What about him?

'He's in Australia, working in the theatre,' she went on. 'It got to the point where he was too old to play the sort of leading parts which had made his name, and nobody offered him the supporting ones because they still thought of him as a star. He was getting no work at all.'

So even if I did manage to claw my way up a bit higher, I knew that it would be no guarantee of security.

Luckily my own predilections offered a way out.

I had fallen in love with the idea of directing TV. I'd always been fascinated by film, and I'd done a certain amount of directing in the theatre, but this seemed to combine the fun of both worlds.

During this time, the early 1960s, we left the days of live drama behind. Everything was recorded. But the reels of two-inch tape were expensive, so it was played straight through as if we were doing a live show, and any necessary retakes done afterwards.

Shaun knew I was fascinated, so he let me sit behind him during camera rehearsals whenever I wasn't needed. The idea of sitting in the gallery, in charge of the whole operation – having worked with the actors in rehearsal; heading the team of designers and production crew; deciding on the camera shots and so on, and making it all happen instantly – seemed to me to be professional paradise, especially if you were directing something you'd written yourself, as Shaun Sutton usually did.

And quite apart from the joy of the work itself, being the director, the Big Daddy of the company, is a sovereign cure for the actor's secret fear – that 'they' are going to find you out, that all your little successes have been down to luck, that after this job you'll probably never work again; and how is it that everybody else seems to have cracked the problem? How is it that all your contemporaries seem to swan from job to job with no sign of the frantic paddling you have to do just trying to keep up?

Of course the real answer, which you know deep down, is that most of them feel just as you do. But try telling that to the scared little mole hiding inside.

Soon after *The Three Princes*, trying to give myself the opportunity to heave myself up the ladder a few rungs, I had written to Michael Barry, the Head of the Drama Department, suggesting that I should do potted versions of well-known books, telling the story from the point of view of the main character, in costume and in front of an appropriate small set.

He asked me to go and see him. I thought at once that we'd get on, as he had a reproduction of the famous Nefertiti bust on his desk, though his was bigger than the one Chummy and I had brought home from our honeymoon in Paris, which still sits in our hall.

'If you're going to have costumes and sets,' he said, 'why not do it as a play? No, I don't think it's a goer. But if you're interested in telling some stories…'

This was a recognised form in those days, long before *Jackanory*: an actor telling a story direct to camera. John Slater was a regular. The slot was the last thing at night, before the BBC closed down at 11pm.

Michael suggested that I should write a six-week series of short stories about life in the theatre, and tell them myself.

It was an extraordinary experience. Live, of course. And I was the only thing on all the British TV screens which were switched on at that time of day.

Apart from one cameraman, one sound man and the floor manager, clutching the script, I was all by myself in the vast black cavern that was Studio D, with two or three blank scenery flats behind me, a potted palm, and a table by the side of my chair, which I was meant to touch casually if I needed a prompt. Autocues? Not even a twinkle in some inventor's eye.

I only needed the table's assistance once, when I was (I hoped) mesmerising the nation with a bit of backstage theatre gossip, and I happened to notice the sound man on his boom absorbed in a copy of the *Evening Standard*.

By the time I'd taken off my make-up, and changed out of the blue shirt – both made necessary by the low efficiency of the cameras, which would flare at a pure white, or a shiny forehead – everybody in the building had gone home, except the night watchman, who let me out into Lime Grove.

There wasn't even somebody to go and have a drink with. In any case, the pubs were shut. I walked to Shepherd's Bush tube and went home.

I had one good notice, from a critic by the name of Maurice Wiggin.

The rest…

But at least I had made contact with a person of power; in fact the most powerful in BBC drama.

So when I first decided I wanted to change direction, in 1960, it was to Michael Barry that I wrote, asking to be considered for a place on the BBC producer/directors' training course.

CHAPTER 5

Round about this time, Owen Holder, an old friend from the York Rep in 1942, who was a well-established television scriptwriter as well as an actor, rang me up to ask me if I'd collaborate with him.

I'd been writing plays and stories since I was six years old but, apart from the *Stage Door* short stories, I'd never had anything accepted. But in the process, I had gleaned quite a lot of know-how. And from our conversations, Owen had picked up on this.

'I've written a story for *Robin Hood*,' he said, 'and they seem to like it. Anyway, they've asked me to write another one. Trouble is, it's been going so long – there've been so many stories already – that I can't think of an idea that's different enough...'

This was the filmed *Robin Hood* series starring Richard Greene. As was revealed much later, the majority of the stories were written under false names by American scriptwriters, some very famous, who had been banned in Hollywood as proto-Communists, as a result of the activities of Senator McCarthy and his infamous Unamerican Activities Committee. But there were always some gaps in the schedule to be filled.

Our story was accepted, but as far as I know never shot. No matter. Here was another source of income, albeit rather sparse. For we went on working together on nearly all Owen's commissions. He paid me one eighth of the fee.

For this, we would get together over two or three evenings and hold a mini brainstorming session, throwing around ideas (sometimes more suited to an episode of *The Goon Show*) until they fell into some sort of structure. I then pulled it together by writing a scene-by-scene breakdown, which Owen would use to complete the finished script. And it went in under his name, which made commercial sense; I was just a backroom boy.

We were a great success as a team. Practically all our ideas were accepted, and the scripts commissioned.

The plums of the scriptwriting orchard were the filmed series, usually American backed, which paid much more than the domestic studio-based drama.

We didn't make *Robin Hood* again, but we wrote a *Danger Man* story – though it probably doesn't appear in the records, as again it wasn't produced; probably because, as always, the producers had to keep an eye on the American market, and we had made a hero of a character based on the contemporary Fidel Castro, kicking out the 'Batista' of a thinly-disguised Cuba. And Owen was asked to do a couple of scripts for *Marco Polo*, another American series; a horse of the same colour, if perhaps from a different stable, as *Robin Hood*.

Now (to strain the equine metaphor a wee bit further), I was by this time chafing at the bit. Any scriptwriter who has been asked to submit a detailed storyline knows that this represents the bulk of the creative work. Writing the actual scenes is relatively a doddle, though admittedly a time-consuming doddle.

Yet Owen was getting seven-eighths of the proceeds.

'Yes, I know it's unfair,' he'd said when I put it to him. 'But I just can't afford to pay you more.'

So we'd agreed that when the opportunity arose, when he was 'in' with a particular producer, he would put my name forward as a possible contributor, so that I could share in the bounty.

We worked out an extra storyline, in addition to the one he'd been commissioned to write, and he took it along, with my name on the title page, and asked the *Marco Polo* producer if he'd be good enough to have a look at it.

He agreed.

After their next script conference Owen asked him about 'my' story.

'Yeah, I read it,' said the man who had his pockets full of lovely dollars, 'It's a good idea. But the guy's got no credits.'

That was that. I was devastated. I'd been so sure that this would be the beginning of an answer to all my problems.

However, it wasn't all that long before another chance came along. The producer of the Granada series *Skyport,* Mike Scott, couldn't get enough of our ideas. We went from commission to commission without a break.

The recording of one of our scripts provides a good illustration of what it was like to work in TV in those days.

As the title implies, *Skyport* was a half-hour series based in an airport such as Manchester, and starred George Moon as a member of an airline's uniformed ground staff, an all-purpose troubleshooter.

This particular story (and this shows how far from today's casual acceptance of air travel we were) featured a businessman (let's call him Banks), booked in to fly to a high-powered conference in Europe. Unfortunately, he's never been in an aircraft in his life, and he's scared to death at the very thought.

So he thinks up the idea of hiding his passport (in the gents) and then pretending that he's lost it, knowing full well that he won't be allowed to check in; and so he won't lose face in front of his colleagues.

It was the custom then (and still is when appropriate) for the producer to invite the writer to attend the recording. So, as usual, Owen went up to Manchester for the day. We happened to be meeting the next evening, to work on the next *Skyport* story.

'How did it go?'

It was practically a routine enquiry by now. The people at Granada knew what they were doing.

'Well, to be honest, I can't think what they're going to do,' answered Owen. 'There's one bit of the recording they just can't get away with...'

This was the time, at the very beginning of the use of the massive Ampex video recorder, when each two-inch tape still cost a great deal of money, or so we were told. It was the policy of every producing company to use the machine simply as a device to freeze in time what was essentially a live performance, hoping that it would be played straight through without the necessity for retakes.

Ian Hendry was playing Banks. Ian was a fine actor, whose naturalistic style was perfectly suited to both TV and film. From playing the lead in the first series of *The Avengers,* along with Patrick McNee, he established himself as one of the most bankable – to use a Hollywood term – of the new stars.

Until alcohol put a stop to his career, and ultimately to his life.

Whether a pre-recording stiffener was to blame we'll never know, but poor Ian was the victim of a cataclysmic 'dry'.

In the scene where Banks goes to the check-in to try to persuade George Moon to let him check in without a passport, he came to a dead stop, right at the beginning of their exchange.

There are dries and dries. The least terrifying (almost routine in weekly rep) is the hiccup when the next sentence slips from your mind, only to be brought back instantly if the actor you're addressing gives you a little clue. Nine times out of ten anybody watching would have no idea that anything had gone wrong.

But the other end of the spectrum is very different.

A total blank. Not only has the particular line disappeared, but also the situation which the scene is portraying; sometimes even the play itself.

In live television the assistant floor manager carried the script in one hand, following the dialogue, and a 'cut-key' in the other, which would cut the transmission of all sound. Without the viewing audience being aware of anything but the strange silence of 'dead air', he or she would give the line, loud and clear. This was how I was prompted in my short story.

But Ian was utterly lost. When it's as bad as this, even to be given a clear prompt is of no use at all. And the consequent rising panic compounds the disaster.

George Moon did his best to help, ad-libbing in character. Unfortunately he didn't think to say, 'What's the matter, sir? Lost your passport, have you?'

'In the end,' said Owen, 'Ian just put his head down, with his hands resting on the desk, and said, "It's no good, I can't go on. You'll have to stop recording."'

But they didn't. And after a long moment he looked up, saw that the red light was still alight on the camera, and managed to pull himself together enough to start ad-libbing himself and fight his way back to the script.

'They didn't do a retake,' said Owen, 'and they can't cut it out, even if they were to sacrifice the tape, because it's all on one shot. There'd be the most horrendous jump. I can't wait to see it when it goes out.'

We didn't have long to wait. It was on air the very next week, and I made sure that I was watching.

Here he comes, the worried Mr Banks. He starts to speak to George, and then stops, his eyes darting from left to right in the beginnings of his panic.

George asks him what the matter is – and then the public address system breaks in…

'Flight Number ZZ 325 to Amsterdam is now boarding. Please proceed to Gate Number Three…' and so on.

While this was going on, we saw George mouthing unheard words; we saw Ian put his head down, with his hands on the desk and say something equally inaudible; and we saw him look up, and start speaking again, just as the announcement finished.

Luckily Banks himself was supposed to be trying to hide an overpowering fear, so what we saw fitted the story. Just about.

Who'd be an actor?

Anybody watching would have thought it was merely a crass bit of bad production. But Granada saved not only the £30 for the tape (yes, that's the enormous sum they cost) but also the overtime for all the crew and cast.

We did so well as regular scriptwriters for *Skyport* that Mike Scott asked Owen to become script editor for the next series, which turned out to be the last.

Owen, quite rightly, thought it would be a sort of nepotism to ask me to write a script for him, but he suggested that we submit a storyline in my name, and that he would give it to Mike, explaining that I was a friend (but had no credits!) and let him decide.

He liked the story, and my script; and asked me to write another.

So now the guy had some credits. I was an actor/writer. Which would have been fine, but for my deadly pattern of procrastination, which, mixed with an optimistic ignorance about how long it would take me actually to write a script, meant that I habitually missed the deadline…

The worst occasion was for Associated Rediffusion, the company that was replaced by Thames Television in the first change of franchises. Six writers were asked to dramatise the short stories of the best-selling author (in the 1930s) 'Sapper', the creator of Bulldog Drummond. Having read all the stories, we had a script meeting at which we were asked which two we would like to tackle; and after a bit of negotiation it was agreed.

'We're working to a very tight production schedule,' said the script editor. 'So it's important that I know just when you can all deliver your first scripts.' And he went round the table getting a personal deadline from each of us.

I plucked a date out of the air which gave me ample time, and went away purring. Two 50-minute shows! Two fees! We'd have a good Christmas after all.

I got on with my life, which included quite a good part in an episode of a detective series called *No Hiding Place* for the same company.

On a cold night shoot on a location in Dulwich, I got talking to the young actor playing the Detective Sergeant. As usual, we started talking about the difficulty of making your name – or indeed of getting work.

He said, 'I know I'm no Olivier. If I could get a regular part in a soap, I'd be happy to stay there the rest of my life.'

Understandable, even though I wouldn't have shared his ambition.

It took him a decade, but he made it in the end.

His name was Johnny Briggs, who retired, dead (the character, not Johnny), from *Coronation Street* in 2006, after playing Mike Baldwin for 30 years.

I enjoyed *No Hiding Place,* because it was so different from everything I'd been doing at the Beeb.

I enjoyed it all the more for knowing that I could polish off the first Sapper story after it was over. I'd already worked out how I was going to tackle it. I'd have loads of time. Ha!

Actors – and directors for that matter – sign their own contracts, but for some reason it is the custom for writers to have them signed by their agents.

Maybe if I'd actually read the contract I'd have saved myself a deal of grief.

Maybe.

While I was rehearsing, I kept getting messages from my agent, Margery Vosper, asking me to get in touch, and I kept forgetting to ring back – or putting it off till later.

The day after we recorded the episode of *No Hiding Place,* I gave her a call.

'Well, thank God you've surfaced at last,' she said. 'They're going mad at Rediffusion. Where's your script?'

I just laughed.

'Oh, they're all the same, these script editors. Don't worry. It's over a fortnight to the delivery date.'

'No, no, no! That's the *final* date, after you've done any rewrites. You should have sent it in two weeks ago.'

Have you ever fainted – passed out? The sort of whiteness behind the eyes which washes over the brain just before you sink back onto the comfortable brick floor is very similar to the feeling I got then.

I don't remember putting the phone down.

It was Friday afternoon. On Monday morning, struggling to hold my eyes open, I delivered the script personally to the office in Holborn.

I wish I could say that this was the last time that anything of the sort happened. There was the horrific occasion of the 50-minute *Emergency – Ward 10* for instance when...

No, no! I can't bear to think of it!

I don't do it these days. I'm a reformed character, m'lud, cor strike me pink if I ain't.

CHAPTER 6

So now I was a writer. But I wasn't a director. Michael Barry turned me down flat.

In an effort to show him that I had the right idea, I'd enclosed a few pages of a sample camera script, complete with a floor plan and camera positions, based on the opening of a stage play I knew well.

'All actors think they can be television directors,' he said in his reply.

'It's much more difficult than it looks. You haven't had enough experience of directing or of television even to be considered. And as for your so-called camera script, don't you realise that it has to be worked out with the actors in the rehearsal room?'

Of course I did. Hadn't I earned my living in television for over five years? The camera script was meant to show that I understood how to structure the shots of a screen play.

In any case, Michael hadn't directed anything himself for some years. The luxuriously lengthy rehearsals the pioneers allowed themselves had been cut back by the ruthless requirements of a demanding schedule. Apart from doing a 90-minute play, which was given a full three weeks, any director who arrived at the first rehearsal without a draft camera script (infinitely changeable) wouldn't last very long.

I wrote back to thank him for his reply, and said that I still intended to be a director, even if it took me ten years.

It actually took six.

I missed an opportunity when BBC2 started in 1964. The BBC advertised for volunteers with television experience to train as directors for the new channel. I didn't hear about it until it was too late to apply.

But by late summer in 1965, the pressures, both positive and negative, were building up.

One sunny Monday morning I was having a coffee in a café near Picadilly circus, relaxing after delivering a script to the Granada offices in Golden Square (why did I have to deliver it in person, I wonder, instead of putting it in the post? Hmmm…).

On the back of an envelope, I wrote down the pros and cons of abandoning acting for directing. Unlike the theatre, television frowned on any attempt to do both.

We'd recently come back from our usual holiday in a hired caravan in a Cornish field. I was physically refreshed – even spiritually in a sense – but mentally in a turmoil. We really shouldn't have gone. Even such a cheap holiday was beyond our means.

I remember overhearing a friend – Johnny Woodnutt – about this time saying to another actor that he'd found that with three children he needed to earn at least £3000 a year to keep afloat. I quite agreed. The trouble was, I was averaging £2000.

And the impulse to direct was getting stronger and stronger. I was reading whatever I could – books like Karel Reisz's *The Technique of Film Editing*, which is a primer of all you need to know (apart from working with actors). I was spending as much time in the gallery as I could wangle. I was itching to sit in that seat, the director's chair.

Huw Weldon, then the big boss of the Television Centre, used to say that there were only two jobs really worth doing in television: director and Managing Director. Well, I was never going to be the latter, so…

The tally of pros was twice as long as the list of cons.

I didn't want to go off at half cock as I had with Michael Barry. So I thought I'd better find out a bit more about it.

Hugh David had had a career very similar to mine, playing a lot of leading parts, especially in children's television. He was part of Rex Tucker's rep, just as I was part of Shaun's. We'd worked together in Cardiff in a TV play written and directed by the very Welsh author Emyr Humphries – who was so Welsh that he'd written the play in Cymric and then translated it into English.

Hugh was one of the BBC2 intake of new directors. So I asked him to have lunch with me and tell me all about it.

In the 'waitress service' of the BBC canteen at the Television Centre in Shepherd's Bush, munching on steak and chips (not bad at all), with a glass of house red (surprisingly good) and surrounded by the buzz of the lucky people who inhabited this world I so desperately wanted to join, I had my first lessons in the reality of life behind the scenes.

'What's it like?' I asked Hugh. 'Is it what you expected?'

'Some ways yes and some ways no,' he replied, 'but I'll tell you one thing. No actor realises just how hard a director has to work.'

And he proceeded to enlighten me.

The Drama Group, whose boss was Sydney Newman (the dynamic Canadian who'd been the 'onlie begetter' of *Armchair Theatre* at ABC), was divided into three departments: Plays, Series and Serials, each with its own

Head, who was *de facto* executive producer of all the shows under his wing. Hugh was in the serials department.

This meant that he, as director, would be responsible either for two episodes at a time of one of the twice weeklies, the soaps, such as (round about that period) *Compact*, *United*, and *The Newcomers*; or taking charge of a complete story which might be anything from six to 12 episodes long.

'If you're on one of the soaps,' Hugh told me, 'you do the two episodes in one week, and then another lot three weeks later, and so on. It's a regular routine, and once you get into the swing of it fairly simple. It's just the production weeks which are a bit of a push. But a proper serial, like a six-part *Doctor Who* – which I'm in the middle of editing...'

'Put it this way,' he went on. 'If you're doing a twice-weekly, it's like running to catch a moving bus. Once you've jumped on, it carries you along for a bit, and then you jump off again. But if you've got a real serial... you've got to push like stink to get the thing moving, and then it starts to run away downhill, and it's all you can do to catch up with it and climb into the driver's seat.'

He laughed. 'A bit fanciful, I know, but it sometimes feels like that. During the actual production weeks you can find yourself working 16-hour days, or even having to work all night.'

'Why?'

'Think about it. While you're rehearsing the actors, you've got to be blocking the cameras for the following week, or you'll turn up at the next rehearsal after the recording without a clue. And you can't do it during the day, because there are planning meetings – with the technical bods and the designers for instance – and if you had some pre-filming, you'll be having sessions with the film editor too – and they've all got to be fitted in somehow. It's literally non-stop.'

'So do you regret having given up being an actor?'

He looked surprised. 'Never in this world. It's all fascinating stuff, and when you manage to get it right, it's like being able to fly.'

Hugh had to go back to his *Doctor Who* after lunch, and he took me down to the editing suite and let me watch the incredibly clumsy process of sticking together bits of two-inch video tape, which entailed the use of a suspension of iron filings and a microscope to match the two halves of the control track, quite apart from having to remove the sound and dub it back on. An edit which nowadays would be achieved with the pressing of a couple of computer keys could take several minutes.

Indeed, on one later occasion I was given a chap who'd only just finished training, and he was so afraid of getting it wrong that each edit was taking over half an hour.

The *Doctor Who* that Hugh was editing was *The Highlanders*, the story which introduced Frazer Hines as Jamie.

I'd worked with Frazer when he was a boy actor, when he played big parts in a couple of Shaun's serials. Seeing him up there on the screen in his kilt confirmed what I'd always thought: that he had a striking personality, and was a good actor as well. It was good to know that he'd got this chance – and he grabbed it with both hands.

Next I approached Owen Reed to ask his advice. He was the present Head of Children's Television, so he knew my work.

'Yes, it is like flying,' he said, when I repeated what Hugh had said. 'Learning to fly an aircraft. You can have all the tuition in the world, but until you go solo you won't know whether you can actually do it or not.'

I told him of my experience with Michael Barry and he said that I would still have to be sponsored by the Drama Group. It was the only way in, apart from starting at the bottom, so to speak, and climbing the assistant floor manager/production manager ladder.

'No, you must go in at your own level,' he said. 'I'd write to Sydney Newman if I were you. Say I suggested it.'

So I did; and got a very friendly letter back from his second-in-command. I can't remember his name. Let's call him Charlie.

'Unfortunately,' Charlie's letter said, 'we've just finished the selection process for the four places available to non-staff. We been through all the applications, and we've whittled them down to 20.

'But I'll make sure that your name is at the top of the list of candidates to be considered for the short list next year. I'll get in touch with you to let you know when we start on it.'

Another year!

Never mind. At least I was in the system. But I knew that I was pushing it; this was in the summer of 1965, which meant I'd turned 40 (what midlife crisis?) and I'd heard that Auntie preferred her suitors to be younger. But I felt that if I was only given the chance, I'd be able to persuade the selection board to make an exception in my case.

I had a good year as an actor, including playing a semi-regular character in the early episodes of *Softly Softly*, and as a writer, being commissioned to write a children's play for Granada and several episodes of *The Newcomers*.

Summer came. But no word from Charlie. Foolishly, I thought it would be bad policy to appear to be pestering him. But as September loomed, I couldn't stand it any longer. I rang the BBC, and asked for Charlie.

When I said my name, there was a horrified pause.

'I forgot all about you,' he said at last. 'I'm sorry, but I'm not with the Drama Group any more. And they've already chosen the 20 candidates, I know.'

I could hardly listen to his apologies. I literally felt sick.

'They had over 400 applications. And the selection board is in two weeks,' he said. 'I'm afraid it's too late to do anything about it.'

'It's not the first time he's done something like this,' said Sydney Newman, 'That's why he's not my deputy any more.'

If Sydney's secretary hadn't fitted me in between his appointments, I think I'd have gate-crashed his office.

'You've got a good case,' he went on. 'We'll make it a short list of 21. Okay?'

It was from this moment that the gods started smiling on me. Perhaps they already had. After all, thanks to Charlie's boob, I'd leap-frogged over the heads of nearly 400 other hopefuls.

And then, at the board itself, having pointed out that I'd filled the gaps in my experience which Michael Barry had singled out – by doing more directing in the theatre, and earning my living for nearly ten years as an actor in television – I was asked if I had any bees in my bonnet (the actual words) about television drama.

This was probably a standard question. Years later, I found myself the other side of the table, selecting candidates for the course. Ken Trodd was one of the other two producers on the board. Both were from the plays department.

The very experienced artistic director of a well-regarded rep was one of the hopefuls. I thought he was obviously what we were looking for. But Ken asked him a version of the same question.

'Is there anything you feel strongly about, that you'd like to have a go at?'

'Well, no,' he said. 'I've directed practically every sort of play in the theatre, and I feel I could tackle anything.'

Just what was needed in the hurly-burly world of series and serials.

But the gentlemen from plays felt differently.

'The chap's got nothing original to offer,' said Ken, in our discussion after he'd gone. 'He's just a journeyman.'

Had I any bees in my bonnet?

'Yes,' I said, 'as a matter of fact I have. I don't think it's a good idea to put plays like _____ (I can't remember the title) in the *Wednesday Play* slot. There's been rather a lot lately. There should be a place for experiments, but I don't think that's it. You'll lose the audience. There's no point in putting on the best play in the world in an empty theatre.'

What I didn't know was that one of the anonymous faces behind the table opposite my chair belonged to Michael Bakewell, the producer of *The Wednesday Play*.

To this day I haven't been able to make up my mind whether I would have said it had I known; but I have a strong suspicion that it was my apparent cheek that swung the decision in my favour!

Auntie – another nickname for the Beeb – had always been a generous old matriarch looking after her littl'uns, and she gave us trainees a six-month contract. After the course, which theoretically fitted us for any department in the corporation (I know how to place the cameras to cover Wimbledon, for example), we had three months in which to try to prove our worth, after which we were either invited into the family (albeit with a short-term contract) or politely shown the door to try our luck in the freelance world.

The dialogue with the selection board had ended thus: 'Have you any questions yourself?'

I'd done my homework. 'No, thank you.'

'Do you know what your salary would be for the six months, if you were taken on?'

It was the one question I'd forgotten to ask Hugh. Or anybody else for that matter. So they told me. Unfortunately the salary for six months was only £750, £250 less than I already knew wasn't enough to get by.

But the gods were still being kind. I managed to fix a commission for a pair of *Newcomers* at £300 a pop. I was in business.

'No man but a blockhead ever wrote, except for money,' said that other famous doctor, Dr Johnson. I strongly suspect that he either said that to shock his hearers (as he so often did) or in a moment of disgust and depression engendered by a spell of what he considered to be hack work. If he had had a modest competence, as a private income used to be called, would he have been content to sit at his dinner table and spout aphorisms? He loved the language too much, surely. Money was secondary.

But having enough money lubricates life. And life in my case means wife, family and friends; storytelling in one form or another; and the perpetual question, 'What's it all about?', as represented by science on the one hand, and religion and philosophy on the other. (Or perhaps that's the same hand, as in 'the sound of one hand clapping'.)

Having enough money. Having too little is nearly as soul-destroying as having too much.

Having started my new career ten years or more later than most TV directors, and at the time of a government credit squeeze, it was many years before I earned enough at the BBC. But the fact that it arrived punctually on the 15th or 16th of every month meant that I was able to drop my concern and concentrate on the things I loved.

I joined on 29 November and I had a ball! The course finished with the joy of recording a 20-minute play as an exercise which I wrote and directed myself – and later expanded for *Thirty Minute Theatre*. It 'starred' Phyllida Law and her husband Eric Thompson, of *Magic Roundabout* fame, whose daughter Emma was only seven-going-on-eight at the time.

While I was having the time of my life, Bill Sellars, the producer of *The Newcomers*, unbeknownst to me, came into the gallery and watched me at work.

And then offered me a job.

But the money gremlins had one more trick up their sleeve. There I was, still working out the last three months of my time as a trainee, on the three-week turnaround of *Newcomers,* and feeling pretty hopeful that I would be offered a two-year contract; and when the time came, I went to see the script editor to get my briefing for the two episodes I was going to write.

'Oh, I've given them to somebody else,' he said. 'That's the BBC rule. You can't write for the same programme you're directing.'

My £600 vanished in a puff of blue smoke.

Now, Shaun Sutton and his wife had become close friends by now, and when I'd told them (while Chummy and I were savouring one of her delectable cheese puddings) that I'd been accepted for the course, he'd laughed and said, 'Shall we tell them, Ba?'

Shaun was about to make an equally dramatic career change; and by the time I was directing *Newcomers,* he'd hung his own pictures on the walls of the office of the Head of Drama Serials.

He'd become my boss.

So I went to see him officially and told him my sad tale.

'Very well,' he said. 'You can write a pair – just two episodes – but you mustn't direct them yourself.'

I think I could have convinced anybody of the justice of my cause, but I can't deny that it can sometimes be useful to have friends in high places.

I was now happily jumping on and off the *Newcomers* bus, and segued smoothly from my trainee contract into two years at 2000 (beautifully regular) pounds a year. We'd just have to manage on that.

CHAPTER 7

Near the converted church at Gosta Green, which was the BBC Television studio in Birmingham before Pebble Mill was built, was a very good bookshop.

This was the thankful bolt-hole to which I escaped during the lunch break on the *Newcomers* recording days. Not that I didn't enjoy the intensive camera rehearsal, but the blessed bookshop quietness – as pronounced as the traditional public library – eased the jangling in my head brought on by several hours of incessant voices, the most insistent being my own.

It was there that I picked up the book that was literally to change my life: *Psychotherapy, East and West* by Alan Watts.

Those who know his writing will have guessed what it was that made such an impression. Alan Watts was an Englishman who was part of a movement which was an integral part of the 1960s' rush of hope for the world, which stretched from the flower-power of the hippies to the LSD experiments of Timothy Leary and Richard Alpert, taking in the Beat Generation of would-be bodhisattvas on the way.

What am I talking about for heaven's sake? Well, maybe it is for heaven's sake that I'm talking.

Eh?

Zen. That's what I'm on about. That was the subject of the Watts book.

I was as emotionally and intellectually turned on as if I was one of Leary's followers myself. Well, no... Perhaps not intellectually – I didn't understand what Watts was describing, but I felt in my very guts that it was nearer to the heart of things than anything I'd ever encountered.

So what's that got to do with the price of lotus-blossoms?

Well, that book started a process, which has become unstoppable, that has given a shape to my life which...

'Now hang on a minute,' I can hear the dedicated fan saying. 'Is this going to turn into some sort of religious tract? I thought this book was going to be about *Doctor Who*?'

Okay, okay.

In the first place, Zen is not a religion.

In the second place, I'm nearly there. Only four episodes of the twice-weekly version of *Z Cars* (the cop show of the day) separates us from the second Doctor, our old friend Pat Troughton, and *The Enemy of the World*.

In the third place, Zen Buddhism was central to the persona of the third Doctor, played by Jon Pertwee – and became more so over the five years before I cast Tom Baker to replace him, culminating in...

All in good time.

The main difference between what I'd been doing in Birmingham and the shooting of *Z Cars* in London – apart from my relish in working in a real studio – was the location filming, my first.

In Studio Four, just as at Gosta Green, I'd be shooting, multi-camera, with giant turreted video cameras with their thick cables. Each scene was played through as though it was going out live, with the shots being instantly edited by a vision mixer, according to a pre-planned script.

Location filming, on the other hand, followed the time-honoured feature film practice of taking one shot at a time on a single camera.

I was going to get to say 'Action!' (rather than 'Cue – and cut!'), like a real live film director. I couldn't wait.

It's a truism that you never stop learning. If you forget that, life is always ready with a smart clip over the ear to remind you.

'But you've got 21 set-ups [camera positions],' said Eddie Craze, my very experienced production manager, when I presented her with my shot list.

'That's right.'

'That's what you'd schedule for a whole day's work. You'd never get away with so many on a night shoot, with all the lighting and stuff. And at this time of the year we'll be lucky if we can start shooting much before ten o'clock.'

I managed to persuade her that it was worth a try. I'd have alternatives up my sleeve if we showed signs of getting behind.

I felt confident that I could make it work. Quite apart from what I'd learnt from books, and from the course, I was going to follow the methods of my real mentor, Shaun Sutton.

Shaun was renowned in the film department for his speed in shooting. And the way he did it was by meticulous pre-planning; editing the sequence in his mind, so to speak (a mental 'story-board'), so that he knew exactly what was demanded of each shot, finding the exact positions for the camera on an early recce, and then accepting the first take, if everybody concerned was happy with it, rather than shooting the 'one for safety' which often multiplied itself alarmingly.

Apart from the speed of actual shooting, my doing it Shaun's way meant that Fred Hamilton, my cameraman, was able to light the whole location in advance, rather than shot by shot.

Eddie had to push everybody, certainly, but by the time the burglar had winded the DI by throwing the swag into his belly, and been caught by the lurking DS, the first glimmers of dawn were only just beginning to extinguish the stars.

'Well? How did I do? That was my first go at directing film,' I said to Larry Toft in the editing suite a couple of days later. Larry had something like 30 years of experience of film editing, both in features and television.

'Have a look,' he said.

He'd assembled the shots exactly as I'd planned, and the whole sequence worked a treat.

I was beginning to feel cocky. 'It seems all right,' I said, trying to hide my glee.

Larry grunted. He was never an effusive man. 'You were very lucky,' he said.

'What?'

'There was no other way of putting those shots together.'

Was he feeling narked because he hadn't had the chance to do a bit of creative editing?

'If any of those shots had been unuseable – and it could easily happen, for a host of reasons – the whole sequence would have been ruined. You must give your editor some alternatives, just in case: covering shots; overlapping the action between the shots; cutaways; that sort of thing. We could have seen the sergeant peeping round the corner, for instance, and I'd have had something to cut to if anything had gone wrong. As it stands, you'd have had to go back for a re-shoot.'

With our tight budget? What a marvellous way to impress my new producer.

So, on the very next pair of episodes, when I found I was shooting on location a conversation between one of the constables and his girlfriend, I made up my mind to get it right.

They were having a picnic, sitting on the grass, and I needed to get a number of different angles, or it would be dull, dull, dull.

The best way to do this would have been to move them about, with their actions reflecting the emotional demands of the scene. Being a beginner, that never crossed my mind. It said in the script that they were sitting on the grass, so that's what I was going to shoot.

So, to please Larry, I covered the whole scene with a very ordinary wide two-shot, and then took a variety of different two-shots (making sure to overlap the dialogue) and a couple of biggish close-ups to end on. Kindergarten stuff.

If it hadn't been for that bloody grass.

In the covering shot, the actress pulled up a stalk, and started chewing it between her speeches. It was a useful prop, and she used it well to help her performance.

So what went wrong?

Continuity, that's what.

She never put it into her mouth, or took it out, at the same moment on each take. Nothing matched.

Again Larry ended up with no option. The only way he could cut the scene together was to abandon all the closer two-shots and stay on the wide shot the whole way through, with the two close-ups tagged on the end like a sudden shout in the viewer's ear.

Everybody's heard of the traditional 'continuity girl' of Hollywood movies. In TV it's one of the multitudinous jobs of the production assistant.

Very few realise how difficult it is, and unless the director, the actors, costume and make-up, the assistant directors and the camera operator take a share in the responsibility for getting it right, it can become just about impossible.

So there I was, established as a director of twice-weeklies. Fine. But I wouldn't feel that Auntie had really taken me in her arms until I'd directed a proper serial.

It was at this point that I was asked to take on a six-parter – and to my delight, it was a *Doctor Who.*

CHAPTER 8

With every fresh project I learnt something new. But on *The Enemy of the World* the learning curve became so steep that I could easily have fallen off.

I've made my feelings about the script very plain; what about the directing?

With the hindsight of 40 years' experience, I'd be hard pushed to award it a B minus or a C – or even to just let it scrape a pass.

That's one snag about recording. You can't let the rosy glow of remembrance fool you. In the age of the video and the DVD, the evidence is there for the whole world to see.

So what went wrong?

Quite apart from my inevitable inexperience, I tried to be too clever.

When I was teaching on the BBC director's course 20 years later I had a refrain, almost a mantra, which I kept repeating: 'Always in the service of the story!'

The story. It's the director's job to tell the story, and to tell it as dramatically as possible. And the best way to do this is via the time-honoured techniques of (first and foremost) the acting, lifting the action to a dramatic intensity, yet keeping it real, and (second) the use of the images and the sound to clarify and heighten the emotional meaning.

If you get it right, the audience won't even be aware of what you're doing.

They'll be swept along by the narrative, lost in the story. Only later, after they've wiped the tears from their eyes, got their breath back after the almost unbearable suspense, stopped clutching their bellies to ease the pain of laughing, only then, in hindsight, should they be able to recognise the skills that have almost literally taken them out of themselves.

Smart-arse quick cutting from shot to shot with no reference to the content of the scene, or the camera wandering aimlessly from character to character as if it has lost interest, do nothing but make you feel as queasy as being on a cross-Channel ferry in a force eight gale.

Or who gives a twopenny _____ (insert expletive of choice) for the fate of the poor idiots trying to blow each other up – in a sequence that cost an indigestible slice of the budget – which happens right at the beginning of the film, before you've even met them, let alone got to know them and care about them?

And as for special effects... It cost a lot, and it's a brill effect, so let's show it again. And again. And again.

Oh dear.

Always in the service of the story.

To give him his due, this is what that fellow Letts was trying to do. But he wanted to open up the sets, make them look twice the size (or, in the case of the caverns of episode five, 50 times the size), bring the action (apparently) into the open air. But...

'This isn't a *Doctor Who* running order,' said the patient Martin Lisemore, looking at the two-page list of recording breaks, scenery changes, model shots, back-projection set-ups (etc etc) I'd given him for the first episode. As production manager/floor manager, he would have the job of making it work. 'It's the running order for a *Wednesday Play*.'

Remember the Wednesday play? The Rolls Royce of drama, with three weeks' rehearsal and four days in one of the big new studios at the Television Centre, with a recording machine available all the time.

'We've got one day's camera rehearsal, and 75 minutes' recording time,' he went on, 'in Studio D at Lime Grove!'

Yes, I cut down. I even persuaded Innes Lloyd, the producer, to give me an extra 15 minutes of recording time.

But it still wasn't enough. Even in the pedestrian episode three that survives, for instance, I held up the recording by moving the flats to make Denes's corridor look longer – and that was the least of it. A sheer waste of time. It had nothing to do with the story.

The inevitable consequence of my mind being elsewhere was the lack of urgency, excitement, drive (call it what you like) that is so evident in the performances and the camera work.

It didn't apply all through, of course. Thanks to Pat, the scenes with Salamander were demanding, dangerous, just as they needed to be.

It wasn't the actors' fault that the rest wasn't up to scratch. They rely on the director to guide them. That's one of his jobs, helping them to find the underlying fear, anger, eagerness, whatever (perhaps through a subtext), that will inform the surface lives of their characters; getting the level of performance right; and whipping up the energy if a scene feels limp.

And the cameras?

A time-honoured compliment to a director or cameraman is, 'Every shot a Rembrandt, mate!'

Well, no, that's not quite what I'm talking about. The framing and the lighting are of course crucial, but it is the sequence of shots, and their dramatic relevance to what's going on in the story (!) that matters most.

It's always easier to make sure of this aspect with the single-camera technique of filming, rather than with the constraints of positioning (and time) that are inevitable with the video multi-camera setup (only used for soaps and sitcoms nowadays), but it can be done. It needs an acute visual imagination, and a lot more pre-planning.

I learnt over the years. But swamping the agonisingly limited time I had for my homework with all the intricate manipulations of the equipment (on the much too small studio floor) that I needed for my grandiose vision meant that the far more important camera work struggled to keep afloat.

Even the big scene where the two Patrick Troughtons confront each other went wrong.

By the time I directed *The Prince and the Pauper* – in 1975, soon after I stopped producing *Who* – the BBC could afford to give me two video machines, so, by recording the two bits in sequence, I could easily make Nicky Lyndhurst's Prince Edward chat to his alter ego in the same shot. But in 1967, the trickery involved had to be done at Ealing as an extra part of pre-filming (another Sunday down the drain. Sorry, Pat).

I thought I knew how. Hadn't I been reading about it for years? How Hollywood did it?

So I asked for a matte box to go on the front of the camera. This held a mask (the 'matte') over one half of the field of view, so that I could shoot Salamander on the left hand side, move the mask over (while Patrick was changing his costume), and then, after winding back the film to the same starting point, take the Doctor answering him on the right hand side.

I'd planned six shots.

'...and cut. Okay, Pat, off you go and get changed.'

Rewind the film. Reverse the matte...

'...and cut.'

One down, five to go.

Long pause. Subdued mutterings in the camera department.

'Sorry, Barry,' says Fred. 'The camera's jammed.'

What?

'You mean I've lost the shot?'

'No, but you're not getting any more.'

Thank goodness I'd got the one.

A week later, I recounted the sad tale to Derek Martinus, the director who was just coming to the end of editing *The Ice Warriors*.

'Why did you do it like that?' he said. 'You could have shot the two sides separately – and the lab would have combined them in the optical printer.'

I'd started reading about the technique of film making so early in life that my state of the art was about 30 years out of date.

At this time, at the end of the day's camera rehearsal, we'd have a final run, the equivalent of the dress rehearsal in the theatre, which would be viewed by the producer and his script editor. And then, as soon as the supper break was called, the director would repair to the little viewing room behind the gallery for a private conference at which the producer gave his 'notes' – detailed reactions and suggestions about the shooting and the acting which he hoped would be taken on board during the recording.

Some producers would use this time to play power games, delivering their opinions as if they were orders from on high, which quite naturally would exasperate an experienced director.

At the end of my second season as producer of *Who*, Chris Barry directed *The Daemons*; and when we came to this moment at the first recording, it was quite clear by his manner that he rather resented my notes.

It wasn't surprising. He had years of directing under his belt. He'd directed the second *Who* story in 1963, for Pete's sake (to use a favourite expression of the Doctor's), the story which had ensured the phenomenal early success of the series: the first Dalek story. Why should he listen to the wafflings of a tyro only a year or so away from being an 'artiste' (as actors were called in BBC jargon)?

After he'd received yet another one of my observations with a heavy sigh (he didn't quite cast his eyes up to heaven) I thought I'd better set things straight.

'Look, Chris,' I said, 'you're doing your job, and I'm doing mine. Somebody has to take the ultimate responsibility, and that's me; but as far as I'm concerned, the producer with the directors is like the pope with his bishops: *primus inter pares* – the first among equals.

'The director has to be thinking of a myriad of tiny details. It's just about impossible to get a broad view of the show, whereas I can sit back and be an audience – but an informed audience. I'm not telling you what to do. I'm here to help.'

After that things were all right between us, and we became firm friends.

Fortunately, back on *Enemy of the World,* Innes Lloyd was of much the same mind as I was when I became a producer. He was always polite, and he kept a firm hand on the reins of his team, Peter and Derrick. If they'd once got the bit between their teeth, wild horses wouldn't have stopped them. (As the BOSS computer in *The Green Death* says, 'I love a really juicy mixed metaphor.')

All the same, with the three of them at it, I was always given so many notes, about shots, cameras and performance – probably all quite valid – that I never managed to get round to delivering them all to those concerned.

But I made sure that I saw all the actors to wish them good luck.

When, before the final recording, I went to Pat's dressing room, he said he wanted to ask my advice.

'They've asked me to sign up for another season,' he said, 'and I really can't make up my mind. It's a real killer, this job. Worse than weekly rep.'

I knew what he meant.

We discussed it for a while, and then I had a bright idea. 'Why don't you suggest to them that the season should be shorter? If they were to do, say, 26 episodes a year, but take the same time to do them as they do to do 40, the pressure would be off – and there'd be time for you to do proper filming as well.'

A moment's thought.

'Great! Great!' he said.

In the event he did say yes, but it was too late to change the schedules, as I might have guessed.

Did Peter and Derrick pick up the idea from him, or did it come to them independently? If it did come from me, I inadvertently did myself a good turn, because it became the structure of the first Jon Pertwee season neatly in time for me to take over. Thank goodness.

After *The Enemy of the World*, I directed a couple of children's serials.

Drama had been taken away from the Children's Department after Owen Reed went back to radio. Internal politics.

And then…

'You like science fiction,' said Shaun. 'Would you like to produce *Doctor Who?*'

What? I didn't give up acting to become a producer. We directors looked on producers as an unnecessary evil. We were the ones that did the actual work, for God's sake.

'You wouldn't have to give up directing,' Shaun went on. 'There'd be nothing to stop you having a go every so often.'

There was one thing to be said for the idea. If I did it for a year, it would get my name known at the Beeb, and I'd be in a much better position for getting jobs as a director…

I'm now convinced that I was asked for two reasons, the first being the cause of the second: Firstly, the viewing figures were so low that the line was in danger of going off the bottom of the graph in the office.

The second reason? Nobody else would take it on. It was being given a last chance. Part of my brief was to find a replacement for the Saturday slot if the decision was taken to dump it.

'Don't tell anybody yet that you're taking over,' said Shaun, when I said yes. 'I have to get the okay from the powers-that-be.'

That meant Sydney Newman, of course.

'I'll tell Peter and Derrick, so you can go and find out a bit more about the programme.'

Peter Bryant had become full-time producer after *Enemy of the World* when Innes Lloyd left but I would be taking over from Derrick Sherwin, who had produced Pat's farewell story, and was the producer of Jon's first, *Spearhead from Space*, Peter having already started work on their next project, the thriller series *Paul Temple.* But they were both still in the *Who* office, and inevitably Peter was still involved.

I was still editing the final episodes of the second children's serial, *A Handful of Thieves* by Nina Bawden, so I was able to trail Derrick and Peter on only a couple of occasions.

I sought them out in the office on Shepherd's Bush Green, and went down to Ealing with them to see the rushes of the previous day's shoot for *Spearhead from*

Space, which saw the Doctor wrestling with what seemed to be a giant condom. It was solemnly agreed that this wouldn't be a satisfactory climax to his fight against the Nestene monster, and would have to be rethought.

On the second occasion, I met them just before lunch in the BBC club at the Centre (the drinking culture of the day meant that a lot of actual work was done in the bar) and heard a jokey account of all the angst they'd been experiencing – a strike at the Centre, which meant that Derek Martinus, much to his delight, had to shoot *Spearhead from Space* on film, entirely on location. And that was it.

Not much of a handover.

Never mind, I thought; when I arrive officially we can spend the first few days discussing the new season.

'Ah, thank God you're here,' said Derrick, who was busy packing the last few odds and ends from the desk into his briefcase. 'If you want to know anything, give us a ring at the Centre.' And off he went.

I stuck my head into the adjoining office, and said hi to Terrance Dicks, the script editor. I'd been introduced to him on one of the earlier occasions, but that was all.

I was the producer of *Doctor Who* – and stayed for five years.

CHAPTER 9

There was one fly in the ointment and it was a big one. Although the new filming schedule gave the actors – and the producer – a breather every so often, it did nothing to take the pressure off the studio weeks.

The cruel turnaround was as relentless as ever for the actors, the production teams and especially the director, whose deadlines approached with the awful inevitability of the rising water in the cellar where the hero of a 19th century thriller serial might find himself trapped.

When I took over as producer on 20 October 1969 it was only three weeks before the location filming for the second story of the season, with Tim Combe as director. *The Silurians* was technically a very difficult show, and I later found out that when we got to the studio stand, on at least one occasion Tim had come to the outside rehearsal straight from working all through the night on his draft camera script.

The Silurians proved to be my baptism by fire. It didn't take long for me to run into real trouble.

You see, in spite of my having done the so-called 'producer's course', it had been far more oriented towards the director's job. Apart from a day working on a fictional budget proposal, we hardly touched on the shape of a drama producer's life. And yet, if it hadn't been for the very real crisis I was soon to be faced with, the programme might never have escaped from the straitjacket of the weekly recording.

It all started off well, though my lack of financial numeracy nearly led me astray.

Sandra Brenholz, who was the producer's and script editor's secretary, had been with Peter and Derrick for a couple of yonks, so she knew the show well, and was an enormous help.

I asked her to persuade the BBC computer (no PCs in those days) to let me have a printout of the current budget, and how it was being spent. It was on my desk waiting for me when I arrived next morning.

I'd already experienced the delights of above and below the line costs (real cash/BBC resources) on *A Handful of Thieves,* which was used as an experiment in a new way of budgeting, so I knew how to interpret it.

For an all too brief moment I was bowled over by an embarrassment of riches. With a budget like this I'd be able to clothe the actors in satin and velvet; have Sean Connery as a guest star; build sets that…

My euphoria collapsed. I'd misread the allocation by a factor of ten. I had one tenth the money I thought I had. Back to earth with a painful bump.

My first positive action as producer came about that same morning. I hadn't been able to get together with Terrance yet, as he had problems of his own. The scripts of the next serial after *The Silurians*, which was called *The Ambassadors of Death*, had run into trouble.

The first episode had been thrown back by the two producers so many times that the writer had given up, so Malcolm 'Mac' Hulke, who had come to the rescue on Pat Troughton's last serial, *The War Games* (but that's another story), played the part of the cavalry yet again.

But even with all his hard-won experience, together with Terrance's rapidly acquired skill as a script editor – he'd joined as Derrick's assistant less than a year before

– Mac would be hard put to it to deliver all six episodes before the director, Mike Ferguson, joined us.

So rather than asking Mac to interrupt his work to come in for a script conference, Terrance had gone to see him, leaving his office, which adjoined mine, to the assistant script editor, Trevor Ray.

Trevor was a jolly bouncing bloke, an actor friend of Derrick's and Peter's, who was hoping to change direction just as I had. He was full of ideas, and was busy at this time finding out whether in principle it would be possible to shoot a serial with the co-operation of the Royal Navy.

I was just getting over the shock of finding out that I was a potential bankrupt at work as well as at home, when Trevor poked his head round the door, lifting his hand to his mouth in a meaningful way.

I had absolutely no idea what he was on about.

'12 o'clock,' he said, as though in explanation.

I still didn't get it.

'At 12 o'clock the sun's over the yardarm…' (well, he had just been talking to the Navy) '…so we move over to the club. It's one of the immemorial customs of the *Who* office.'

'Well, it's always possible that the custom might change,' I said, still engrossed in my printout.

A beat. (That's what's put in a script to indicate a tiny pause.)

The door gently closed.

I felt better. I was in charge after all.

I hardly got to meet Jon Pertwee before we started the rehearsals for the studio. I visited the unit when they were on location, and hated having nothing to do but watch instead of being in the thick of the action.

It took me quite a while to realise the value of these visits to the filming by the producer. Hang around for a while, and you'll find that somebody who is standing next to you apparently by accident obviously wants to say something.

A heavily edited example (not from *Who*):

The make-up designer, for instance. Let's call her Mary.

'I expect you've heard about the wig row...'

'No, tell me?'

And out it'll come. How Humpty Dumpty, the well-known actor who is playing the important small part of a bald farmer – bald in the script: essential for the action – had refused to take off his toupée, on the grounds that nobody knew that it was false, and how he had insisted that they put a bald wig over the top of it, and how the director had refused to shoot the scene, telling Mary that it looked ridiculous and...

How do you sort that one out? Mr Dumpty is an old man with a prestigious name in the theatre. But you have a peep at him, sitting in the lunch tent doing the *Daily Telegraph* crossword, and, yes, it does look ridiculous.

A conference at lunchtime with the director and the lighting cameraman.

Move the scene from the farmyard into the darkness of the barn? Well...

This is a fictitious story. But I assure you that it's based on fact, and if I told you the name of the actor... He's dead now, but even so I wouldn't be so cruel.

We had a drink together after the first recording, Jon and I. He obviously felt a bit lost since Derrick had disappeared. He'd relied on him a lot for advice, while he was looking for the character of the Doctor.

Jon had started as a straight actor, going into weekly rep after drama school, as so many of us did, but he'd made his name in comedy, especially in radio shows – *Waterlogged Spa*, for instance, and *The Navy Lark*.

In *Spearhead from Space*, especially in the first episode, he felt he'd been searching for his 'green umbrella', as he explained to me. This is a reference to an anecdote in a book by Stanislavski, the Russian founder of the Method school of acting later espoused by Marlon Brando and so many others. In the book, an actor can't find a way into the reality of his character, until one day he marches into rehearsal triumphantly brandishing a green umbrella he's seen in a shop window. Now he can start.

A lot of actors need this approach. Beryl Reid, for example, always said that she was lost until she found the right shoes. Laurence Olivier would have agreed that his reliance on false noses and other make-up tricks was his version of the green umbrella.

By the time he got stuck into *The Silurians*, Jon had found his. Surprisingly, it was his own personality. The elegance of the dandy, the air of authority and, yes, the charisma, all these were facets of himself.

But he still needed reassurance; and he was gratified to find that I had been an actor for over 20 years, so that I knew what he was talking about.

Over the next five years I got to know him well.

But self-centred? Manipulative? Over-sensitive?

Self-centred… I have a vivid picture in my mind of an occasion when we were on a brief location which hadn't warranted our employing a location catering van, so we'd all repaired to the local pub for lunch (on Auntie, the generous old soul). I happened to notice Jon sitting in the corner surrounded by most of the cast, who were roaring with laughter. So I joined them.

Jon was on very good form, pouring out a stream of anecdotes from his past. Very funny they were too. But every tale had the same hero.

This wasn't a one off. His stories were always worth listening to. Mind you, as you heard his favourites again and again over the years, you realised they were being constantly edited – possibly unconsciously, possibly not. They always referred to a real occasion, but if you'd been there, as you listened you came to realise how extraordinarily unaware you must have been not to realise at the time that it was Jon who'd come out on top.

He was always able to trump a story. I once broke three ribs, falling onto the edge of the bath when I was papering the wall above it (bloody fool). When I told Jon, he said, 'Mm. Very painful when you cough. I broke a couple of ribs once.'

'How?'

'Oh, I fell off a camel in Picadilly.'

Manipulative... Very early in our acquaintance, I was in my office one morning when I had a call from Jon.

'Trouble I'm afraid, Barry. I've got a gammy leg – a cartilage that slips out. When it happens I can't even bend my knee.'

'Are you at the rehearsal rooms?'

'No, I'm at home. I'm not needed until two o'clock. But you see, the only person who can fix it for me is my doctor; he's also a trained osteopath. I've given him a ring and if I can get over to him he can fit me in.'

It appeared that the doctor had his practice about five miles away from Barnes, where Jon lived.

Now what would you do in those circumstances? I know what I'd do. I'd ring for a taxi.

Not Jon.

'Do you think you could organise a BBC car to pick me up?' he went on.

Well, maybe this is what 'stars' expect... So I ring Transport and get a car, go to his house, escort him to the doctor and back to Barnes. Well, I have got to make sure he's fit for rehearsal, and the recording at the end of the week, haven't I?

But only a week or two after this, he asks me if I could get permission for him to have a photocall in the grounds of the Television Centre. It was for a leaflet advertising a charity 'do', and the shots would feature a young lady, a patron of said charity, dressed in Edwardian costume to match the Doctor's.

Oh, and by the way, could he borrow Bessie, the Doctor's little yellow car?

With some difficulty I got permission from the always tricky Centre management – it was for charity, after all. And I arranged for Bessie to be driven over from Kingsbury, where she was kept.

But who was to be there to represent the programme and the BBC, to make sure that nothing went wrong? I could hardly ask any of the production teams; my secretary had to man (woman?) the office; there was only one person available.

This is often the way. When camera rehearsal was too fraught to allow a break, Graeme Macdonald, when he was the producer of *The Wednesday Play*, had been known to turn up with a tray of tea for everybody in the gallery.

The shoot went well. The beautiful young lady with the parasol was escorted by her mother, elegant and skinny, with an accent that spoke of cucumber sandwiches on the lawn overlooking the lake. It was obviously a society 'do', this charity 'do'.

When it was over, Jon had another request. He was going home in costume, but would it be possible to find a dressing room for Lavinia to change in?

Of course.

As the surprised girl in Reception was making the requisite phone calls, Lavinia's mum turned to me, her perfectly manicured hand hovering over her handbag.

Good grief! (another of the Doctor's euphemisms) She was going to give me a tip!

'Let me see,' she said, 'You are Mr Pertwee's… er…?'

'I'm Mr Pertwee's employer,' I said. 'I'm the producer of *Doctor Who.*'

It was surprising how her manner changed. Suddenly I was, if not an equal, somebody it might be worth cultivating.

This was the last time I joined in the game. If I was to retain my authority, it had to stop.

Maybe *I* was being over-sensitive.

And maybe not.

By the time Jon had finished his five years, Terry Walsh, his stunt double, was also doubling as Jon's masseur; Michael Wisher, one of our regular actors (who later played Davros in *Genesis of the Daleks*) had done a considerable amount of carpentry and decorating (his standby job as a freelance actor) at the house in Barnes; and John Levene (aka UNIT's Sergeant Benton) had chauffeured him all over the country to his various extracurricular activities.

Don't misunderstand me. I'm not suggesting that Jon exploited them. Terry and Mike were glad of the extra money, and the advice and confidence that Jon gave John were the foundation of his subsequent successful career as an entertainer.

And over-sensitive… By this, I don't mean that he easily took offence, though he could become very irritated if he thought that he was being sidelined in any way. But then that was probably nothing but a symptom of what I am talking about. In Jon, maybe, the actor's vulnerability was at an extreme.

Jon came from a theatrical family. His mother, his father and his brother were all actors, as was his cousin, Bill Pertwee; and his father, Roland Pertwee, was also a very successful playwright.

But Jon told me that he'd always been the butt of their jokes. Expelled from more than one school, he was no academic; but even though his theatrical abilities soon became evident in the school play it seemed that, when he left, nobody took his ambition to follow in the family footsteps seriously. His father in particular didn't try very hard to hide his disbelief in his son's talents.

So when Jon found himself playing a really cracking leading part in the Brighton rep, he went home to London on the Sunday before the first night especially to ask his father if he would come down to see him play.

'If I can, if I can,' was the reply.

Every night, as the auditorium filled up, Jon peeped through the stage manager's spy hole to see if he could spot his father, and on the Friday night...

Yes! There he was! No mistaking him.

That night Jon gave the performance of his life.

As the cast took their curtain call, he tried to see if his father was applauding, but the spotlights blinded him. So he'd have to wait until his dad came round backstage, to his dressing room.

He waited and waited; and his father didn't show up.

So the next day he rang him up to ask him what he thought of his performance.

'What? Oh, sorry. I couldn't get there. Too busy,' said his father.

When Jon, now a man of over 50, told me that, he had tears in his eyes.

CHAPTER 10

So what was the deep doo-doo I soon found myself wading in?

Apart from the radical alteration of the scheduling, *Doctor Who* was part of another enormous change. BBC1 was going into colour, following its successful launch by David Attenborough as the Controller of BBC2.

Apart from the filmed locations, *The Silurians* was to have the luxury of being shot in the wide open spaces of the Television Centre studios, with their brand new colour cameras, rather than in the cramped old relic of the 1930s that was the ex-Gainsborough studio in Lime Grove.

This meant that Barry Newbery, the designer, could stretch his wings and fill the seven studio stands with everything the show demanded, including the massive caves in which the Silurians had been living since prehistoric times.

Or did it?

I'd walked into a colossal row.

Scenic Services, who looked after the actual making, storage and transport of the sets, and Studio Management, who had the job of putting them up before the show and striking them afterwards, necessarily worked in close conjunction, and when Barry sent in his construction plans Studio Management blew up.

'You're categorised as a small drama. We haven't the manpower to set as much as this overnight. You'll have to stick with the amount of scenery you had at Lime Grove!'

Peter and Derrick, as *de facto* co-producers, were understandably outraged, and after a number of increasingly acrimonious meetings, a compromise was reached: at Barry's suggestion, instead of shooting each episode in sequence, all the scenes in the caves would be shot on one day, with the sets filling the studio, and edited in afterwards. This would be heavy, certainly, but would have to be set on only one occasion; and also it would mean that they didn't have to be saved, with the risk of damage.

As a *quid pro quo*, Barry took a leaf out of Orson Welles's book. In *Citizen Kane*, running out of money just when he needed to build the grandiose interiors of Kane's Xanadu castle, his designer faked it by designing immense set pieces (that ludicrously large fireplace, for example), with Gregg Toland, the lighting cameraman (a genius in his own right), losing the background in dramatic darkness.

So Barry did the same with the rest of the underground sets, achieving a really impressive result with a minimum of construction.

So what went wrong?

Firstly, the stew was still simmering on the back burner, all ready to boil over when the sets for *Ambassadors of Death* came up.

Secondly…

'I've been down to look at the cave sets,' said Barry on the phone, 'and they're way behind with making them.'

The rocky caves would normally have been constructed with a chicken wire base, to give the right basic shape, covered with hessian and plaster; but the outside firm that had taken on the job told Scenic Services that the modern way, using fibreglass resin (like building a boat), would be much more effective.

'They don't seem to know what they're doing. You'll be lucky if they're ready,' he went on.

As you can imagine, he didn't have time himself to keep chasing them up. He was far too busy coping with the rest of the sets.

Right. A job for the producer. I got onto Scenic Services straight away.

'Not to worry,' said the bloke in charge. 'I'll get down there right away.'

We'd been told on the producer/director course: don't arrive too early on the camera day. It's not fair on the designer, who'll still be coping with the inevitable problems. And the designer, in the same way, won't want to bug the crew who are putting up his sets.

So it wasn't until about seven o'clock in the morning on the day of the caves that Barry rang me at home.

'I warned you,' he said. 'There's only about half of it here and most of that's unuseable. You haven't got a studio.'

Let's face it, it was ultimately my fault. I'd now learnt the hard way one of the first rules of producing: always check up in good time. And keep checking.

But what to do about the non-existent caves?

This was a crisis of some magnitude which could cost the Corporation a great deal of money.

The BBC at that time was (and possibly still is, in spite of the cuts) the largest TV production organisation in the entire world – oh, yes, including the large American networks. All possible resources were thrown our way. Chippies, painters, scene painters, construction crews, everybody and anybody who might be able to help, swarmed into our studio, having been taken off all but essential work.

Under the direction of Barry Newbery and Tim Combe, who might have understandably thrown in the towel and gone home, half a studio-full of caves was created out of virtually nothing; and after lunch shooting began.

We still had to have a half-day's remount later on, and the post-mortems were painful; but looking back, taking it as a whole, I think it's a story of BBC success rather than failure.

When I was first an actor in television, knowing that we were the pioneers in something which could grow and develop just as theatre developed from its beginnings in Athens, I used to say, a bit loftily perhaps, 'We're the Ancient Greeks of TV drama'.

Well, not all that long ago, I thought I'd lived through the whole cycle.

I looked back on the totality of the time before the satellite stations and the digital explosion, when we had just the four channels (not to mention the Johnny-come-lately Five), and I felt I was looking at the Golden Age, even allowing for the ration of rubbish seemingly inevitable in any schedule.

More almost always means worse. The fragmentation of the audience, the spreading thin of resources and talent, seemed to have made it inevitable that populist 'reality' programmes and cheap makeover shows (whether of gardens, houses or human beings) should come to dominate the schedules.

The BBC I knew was a powerhouse of talent and experience. Since John Birt, as Director General, drained away so much of its creative energy with his management-speak and redundancies, it had been in danger of becoming nothing but a publishing house, commissioning independent producers on the Channel 4 model.

But since he left, there has undoubtedly been a swing in the other direction. There have been some remarkable programmes, including drama made 'in house', such as *Bleak House*. And in some respects they can be better than ever. Nobody, for example, with any sensibility at all can fail to acknowledge what Russell T Davies has done to rejuvenate *Who*.

The majority of those working in commercial television are as keen to produce quality programmes as anyone at the Beeb, but the fact remains that it is the long-established public service ethos of the Corporation, plus the independence that the licence fee gives it, which will always tend to keep the standard high across the board.

That independence, so hated by Governments of every complexion, must be maintained. If the BBC were to be forced to go commercial, or to dilute the licence money by sharing the public service remit with the other terrestrial channels, as has been suggested, it would inevitably lead to a near-total 'dumbing down'.

We must be the watchdogs, and howl a warning if we see any minister approaching with evil intent, however disguised by calling it liberalisation, or privatisation, or whatever cant word is fashionable at the time.

Where was I?

Oh yes, the row with Studio Management about the heavy number of our sets.

One of my mottoes in life is (and was): Never turn a crisis into a confrontation; or only as a last resort.

Sympathy and compassion may not appear to be appropriate words to apply to the job of humping around bits of scenery. But when you think what they mean…

Though they have come to be subtly different (compassion seems to imply an urge towards action, rather than the full-hearted but passive emotion of sympathy) they derive from similar roots, one from Latin and the other from Greek, meaning a 'with-feeling', or perhaps you could say a 'feeling with' i.e. putting yourself in the other's place.

This is no small matter. George Bernard Shaw used to talk about 'the moral passion' that is in-built in humans, quite apart from any religious connotation. Nowadays we might say that it's written into our DNA, probably as a survival ploy through natural selection.

You don't believe me? You have a conscience, don't you, that firmly lets you know whether you're doing the 'right' thing? When we read of the way those who lack a conscience behave – the psychopaths, the sociopaths, the ones with a 'personality disorder' – we can hardly believe they belong to the same species as us.

This is the clue. The moral passion can easily be corrupted, twisted to fit an artificial ideology (Nazism for example), or constrained by a set of rigid (usually religious) rules. But the basis of true morality and ethics lies in our recognition that the child with a swollen belly and flies crawling into its eyes in Ethiopia, or the drunk lying in the gutter in danger of freezing to death, or the widow clutching her belly in an agony of grief because her whole family has been wiped out by an Israeli bomb (or a Hezbollah rocket), are our brothers, our sisters.

This has nothing to do with Churchianity or the equivalent in the other religions (including Buddhism). I'm talking about simply recognising the way things are.

The existentialists made great play with the idea that each of us is ultimately alone in the world. But this is surely wrong. Our very existence is inextricably bound up with that of our fellows – and this becomes even more true if we include the rest of the natural world, including the insects and the plants.

Terrance once laughed at me when I told him that a fly was his cousin.

'A monkey, maybe,' he said. 'Or even a dog. But a fly?!'

Why, yes. If evolution is true, as I believe (on the basis of the evidence, not because of faith in the pronouncements of the scientists), it's likely that all living things share a common ancestor, even if that was a single-celled creature like an amoeba.

So what has all this got to do with *Doctor Who* (and his scenery)? Everything.

To start with, this way of thinking underpins all the stories that Terrance and I had anything to do with. One of the strengths of *Doctor Who,* when it is true to itself, is its grounding in the eternal myth of the hero – the flawed hero – who is plainly on the side of right, fighting evil and emerging the victor.

The sort of anti-hero whose only difference from the villain is a bigger fist, who will cheerfully break any rule if it means that 'his' side wins the game of life and death, may have a place, but it certainly is not in *Who.*

The Doctor, if he is to be true to himself, must be more humane than many a human.

The very first time I changed a line was in the final scene of *The Silurians*, not long before they actually shot it.

As was his way, the Brigadier had solved the problem of the reptilian creatures who had survived from prehistoric times by blowing up their world of caverns and effectively finishing them off.

The script went something like this:

```
DOCTOR: That was a stupid thing to do. They
were a very advanced people, in many ways
far beyond the human race.

Just think what we might have learnt from
them!
```

Wrong... I changed it to:

```
DOCTOR: That's murder! They were intelligent
alien beings - a whole race of them. He's
just wiped them out...
```

And the Doctor turns away, deeply moved.

Compassion. People shy away from the word, with its touchy-feely do-goody modern ambience. But it makes utter practical sense.

Never turn a crisis into a confrontation.

Compassion. *Feeling with...*

'I wouldn't have your job for all the tea in China,' I said to Jim, the one from Studio Management who was in charge of the overnight scene-setting crews.

He visibly relaxed.

I had set up a meeting with everybody who might be concerned: Jim obviously; Ronnie Marsh, who had taken over as Head of Serials when Shaun was promoted to be Head of the Drama Group; and the heads of the relevant departments in Design, Scenic Services and Studio Management. And probably a few more. I wanted it to be as comprehensive as possible and solve the problem for good.

I meant what I said to Jim. Just think. Not all the eight studios would have to be set overnight, certainly; some would have been out of operation, or have had a day set. But because of the high turnaround, it was very usual that the settings for a particular show would have to be struck, and those for the next day brought in to replace them overnight.

Like everybody else at the BBC (and probably in every organisation in the world; did somebody mention the NHS?) Jim would find himself with barely enough resources to get the job done. It would need considerable juggling of the various components of the crews to make sure that it all worked.

The big snag was that, as in Parkinson's law (every job expands to fill the time available), every producer, director and designer would quite rightly be trying to squeeze the utmost juice out of their own bowl of fruit.

Speaking of bowls of fruit… When I started directing *EastEnders* in 1990, I tried to get rid of the bowl of fruit in the Fowlers' sitting room. Wendy (Pauline Fowler) went beresk [sic], as they used to say at the Beeb. How was I to know it was her own personal talisman – and was to stay there (with sufficient changes of fruit) until Pauline's dramatic death 17 years later?

Too much scenery. So what could be done about it?

We talked round and round, coming up with various off-the-wall ideas without getting anywhere, until Jim brought us back to reality by pointing out the simple fact that it all went wrong when the number and complexity of the sets was larger than expected.

So I suggested that the way forward was to give everybody more information about our intentions much earlier on. The designer would discuss his plans with Studio Management and Scenic Services before finalising them and sending them off for construction. This was agreed; and with a sigh of relief everybody started to pick up their things to get back to their real work.

And then I threw in a remark (which I didn't expect to be taken seriously) which opened the whole thing up again.

CHAPTER 11

Nearly ten years before, I'd been in a dramatisation of a Trollope novel *The Small House at Allington.* We did it in six weekly half-hour episodes. It turned out to be the most comfortable live show I was ever in.

You see, the producer/director Michael Leeston-Smith, who I think came from radio, had a fantastic idea. We started rehearsals a week earlier than usual, and then each episode rehearsed for two weeks rather than one: Episode A in the morning and Episode B in the afternoon; then Episode B in the morning and C in the afternoon; and so on.

The difference it made was phenomenal. There was time to learn the lines properly; and Michael had ample opportunity to work out his cameras.

This is what crossed my mind as we finished the meeting, and I blurted my thought out loud.

'I just wish we could do two episodes a fortnight rather than one a week,' I said. Ronnie Marsh pricked up his ears. He'd been producer/director of *Dixon of Dock Green* for several years with the same murderous schedule.

'What do you mean?'

'Well... we'd only have to put the sets up once, instead of twice.'

The head of Scenic Services (Harry, wasn't it?) actually laughed, but not in derision.

'I've been trying to float that for years,' he said, 'but I've never been able to find a producer willing to have a go.'

So I wasn't the only one who thought the present system was madness.

Barry Newbery, the designer of *The Silurians,* has also said that he mentioned the possibility to me after the debacle of the caves; though I don't remember it.

It's obvious once you take a good look at it, like all really good ideas.

TH Huxley, the top biologist who was Darwin's main champion, said of his theory of the origin of species, 'How extremely stupid not to have thought of that!'

And think of the safety pin! Centuries of pricked fingers; and then: 'Why didn't I think of that!'

Jim, in particular, welcomed the idea like a long-lost son; it solved the scenery problem at a stroke. If we were only to have one set-up and one strike instead of two we could fill the studio with as many sets as we liked.

It was too late for *Ambassadors of Death,* but we made it by *Inferno.*

The sighs of relief from the actors and the production teams could be heard in Newcastle.

But we weren't quite out into the open sea yet. With only two and a half hours' recording time on the second studio day to record both episodes, it was still a frantic scramble to get the show on tape, as I found out for myself when I directed *Terror of the Autons* at the beginning of the next season.

What's more, it made it very difficult for the cameramen, doing two on the trot, because they had to remember their early moves from the previous morning.

But then Mike Briant, when he directed *Colony in Space,* asked for an extra short recording on the first day, nominally for special effects – and once the precedent was established, I was able to extend the earlier recording to two and a half hours as well, so that we could do one episode per camera day, with double the recording time.

All the extra angst, grief, stress, call it what you will, disappeared and we were left with nothing but the normal impossibility of all television production.

With one bound our hero was free from his waterlogged cellar – and the fly climbed out of the ointment and started to wash its face.

Dear old Jon. Well, not so old then. He was only 50 years old when I joined.

Thinking of those early days, when each recording was like a first night rather than a filming session, conjures up a picture of Jon before the recordings of *The Silurians*, sparkling fresh from make-up and resplendent in his flowing cloak and frilly shirt, gathering the other members of the cast around the microphone in the opening set, and conducting them in a strange chorus.

Most actors, before going on for their first entrance, will go through some sort of warm-up. Indeed, nowadays some more intense theatre directors will insist, every day, on the whole company joining them for anything up to an hour to go through physical and vocal exercises together. The usual result is an exhausted cast, especially on matinee days with two shows.

However, many will at least lubricate the vocal cords – and I don't mean with a double Scotch, though it might be said that that's another fairly common way of going about it. I'm talking about lubricating the cords with some exercise from their voice-training days.

Jon, being Jon, had his own idiosyncratic way.

Just before half past seven, when the recording was about to start, the studio would ring with a chorus of voices (the entire cast), led by Jon's, with the resonance of a Pavarotti, chanting the mystic words, 'HARRY RO-O-O-OY…'

Harry Roy? Who he?

Harry Roy was a well-known band-leader in the 1930s, when Jon was growing up.

In the end, Jon must have realised that all the younger members of the cast were equally mystified, and so later on he changed the name that boomed out of the loudspeakers.

Tim Combe, after he'd retired from directing to become an actors' agent, would have had a surprise in store if he ever visited a recording session.

'Stand by on the floor,' the director would say into his mike in the gallery at one minute to 7.30, to be answered by the even more sonorous name resounding through the studio in chorus:

'TIM CO-O-O-O-MBE…'

Even before Mike Ferguson joined us as director of *Ambassadors of Death*, and had been presented with a full set of scripts (thanks to the efforts of Mac Hulke), Terrance and I had to get cracking with ideas for the last story of the season.

Don Houghton, who was very experienced in the world of TV series, and who later became one of the writers (and later still the story editor) of the Hammer Horror films, had come to Terrance with an intriguing fact he'd found.

The Americans had, not all that long ago, started a massive scientific project – which may have been inspired by Conan Doyle's Professor Challenger story, *When the Earth Screamed*.

They set up a drilling rig way out to sea with the intention of boring through the Earth's crust to the deliciously named 'Mohorovičić discontinuity', to find out what lay beyond.

How far they got we shall never know, because they abruptly stopped drilling – and when Don tried to find out the details, he was told that the information was top secret. Why?

No matter how much he ferreted around, he couldn't get to the bottom of the mystery. Were they covering up some dreadful calamity? Or had they let loose upon the world a horror beyond the imagining of a Stephen King or a Dean Koontz, and were desperately trying to keep it under wraps?

This was how *Inferno* was born. In a couple of script conferences the three of us thrashed out the basic story of the 'Mohole Project'.

As it stood it would have made a great four-parter.

The curse of Episode Five had come upon Terrance and me early in our work together. Unless you introduced a new story element (probably with expensive new sets or extra actors), Episode Five – in a six-parter – was apt to degenerate into a chase-about through interminable corridors, with the development of the story marking time until the grand dénouement in Episode Six. And we had seven weeks to fill.

The answer might seem obvious: Just make a four-parter and get somebody quick (Mac Hulke?) to write us a three-parter to finish the season.

But we were already badly overspent. We just couldn't afford any extra sets, costumes, monsters…

It was Terrance who came up with using the idea of a parallel universe.

Brilliant. Same sets, same actors; and an opportunity for our regulars to have a bit of fun. Nick Courtney's fascistic Brigade Leader with his piratical eyepatch, and his sidekick Carry John's dominatrix, not to mention the nasty specimen John Levene made of Benton's transformation, gleefully gave us three completely new characters. Buy one get one free, so to speak.

The scripting of *Inferno* was going on even before *Ambassadors of Death* went into production. The programme would have been in the same trouble as so often before if Terrance and I hadn't got on with it.

Trevor Ray had been brought in by Derrick and Peter as a possible future script editor more compatible with their freewheeling style when it became apparent that Terrance (much as he got on with Derrick – an old colleague from *Crossroads* where he got his start in TV) was quite likely to relinquish his contract.

Luckily he and I had very much the same attitude to the work as each other, and he decided to stay – and Trevor decided to go and join his soulmates on *Paul Temple.*

No matter what you may have heard from other sources, there's no question that there was a strong possibility that Season Seven, when I took over, would be the last. Even Shaun Sutton in the odd interview has denied this, which is odd because, as I told you, it was Shaun himself who asked me, as part of my brief as producer, to come up with a programme which could if necessary replace it in the 'family' slot it occupied on Saturday evening.

Right from the start of the BBC in 1923 it was always the job of the producer to be the conduit for new ideas for programmes, whether they came from outside writers, colleagues in the Corporation, or from the producer himself.

I came up with one, for a 45-minute series/serial in 13 parts – which curiously enough is the very format of the modern reincarnation of *Who* – and I still think it could have been a goer.

It was called *Snowy Black*, the name of the hero – a large and ebullient drover (Australian cowboy) from the outback who comes to 1970 London on the trail of a lost family fortune. An innocent abroad, tangling with the complexities of urban sohistication. A bit like *Crocodile Dundee,* perhaps, but of course this was years earlier.

It was good enough for the Powers-That-Were to commission a pilot script, and put the recording of a pilot episode into the schedules; and I was allowed to write it myself because I wanted to tailor it to the use of multiple video cameras on location, using up to three at a time as in the studio, which would allow for many more exterior scenes. By limiting the number of locations I hoped to be able to shoot as much as a third to a half of each episode outside.

This may not sound a very revolutionary notion; and I wasn't the only one keen on it. But in 1970 it had hardly been tried.

This was largely because the introduction of the portable video camera was some time in the future. In 1976 we shot *Little Lord Fauntleroy* entirely on location with the new small ones. But in 1970 we would have to use the overgrown Outside Broadcast cameras that belonged to the Sports department, along with assorted support vehicles each the size of a large pantechnicon.

I got the go-ahead for the pilot at the end of November 1969. Our last recording of the serial which turned out to be *Inferno* was to be on 29 May 1970, and we were to plunge straight into rehearsals for the OB shoot.

I wrote a sample scene to cast the most important part, and found an Aussie actor, Mark Edwards, who was really enthusiastic about the project (as well he might have been. The lead in a new series? I'd have given my eyeteeth for a chance like that a few years before. Well, perhaps not. I still haven't got dentures 39 years later).

The rest of the casting would have to wait, if only because I hadn't finished writing the script – and I was in grave danger of running into the same old trouble, a late script. But this time the deadline was unchangeable, and I was the one delivering the manuscript to the director, who happened to be me.

I had no time to write during the day. I was far too busy with the current productions; planning the next season with Terrance; setting up the team which would be working on *Snowy Black* with me and so on. So I was writing at home in the evenings – and would have inevitably ended up with more of the only too familiar all-night sessions.

It gives me the instant collywobbles even to think of it.

And then, in April, because of the great success of the new *Who,* the project was cancelled (poor Mark).

I was saved by the bell. And as they did for Mark, they even paid me my full fee.

CHAPTER 12

I doubt if I would have stayed on *Who* for over five years if I hadn't met Terrance Dicks. And, as I told you, he was halfway to leaving when I arrived.

We soon discovered that we looked at the problem we'd had dumped in our laps in very much the same way. But it was more than that.

Simply put, each of us understood what the other was saying.

If you're as interested in the use of words as I am, and if it's an integral part of both your professional and your personal life, inevitably your vocabulary grows; and grows; and grows; and you find that you are quite naturally using words that are not normally bandied about in conversation.

The very old cliché, The University of the World, wouldn't quite apply to my further education. My surrogate colleges were the public library and, more than I could afford, the bookshop.

Over the years I would regularly become obsessed by different topics – no, that's too limited a word – different areas; and I would read everything I could lay my hands on which was remotely relevant – and sometimes have a go at those with a practical application.

At one time or another I have become a temporary – and undoubtedly mostly superficial – 'expert' in: drawing; portrait painting; animation; stage and film make-up; sculpture in clay; mask making; puppets;

optics (3D projection without glasses); human physiology; cosmology; ecology; organic gardening; philosophy; psychology; religions (especially those of the East); simple electronics…

The last was an offshoot of a long-standing fascination with musical instruments. I read everything I could find, and tried to create new sounds by the application of musical acoustics in untried ways.

Have I missed any? Oh, yes. Trying to find a successful horse-race betting system to cure my chronic disorder: lack of money.

I spent the whole of the summer of 1954 going through the form books of previous years, either testing systems which I'd bought, or trying to spot ways of creeping under the barriers of the bookies' own infallible system, the 'over-round' scale of odds.

You see, I know the jargon. I understand it, too; enough anyway to be able to suss out the scam in most offered systems. Given time, I could construct a system which could be checked from the form books over, say, the last ten years, coming out with a chunky profit year on year, which would fool 90% of punters.

I think I have in fact found a way of beating the odds at roulette. Impossible? Yes, of course it is. The odds are openly rigged in favour of the bank.

I'm talking about spotting the idiosyncratic bias of a particular wheel, with a particular croupier in charge, using the built-in (and largely unconscious) expertise of the human brain.

So why haven't I broken the bank at Monte Carlo?

Because I can imagine nothing more boring than sitting at a roulette table for just one evening, let alone making it my life's work.

Yes, I can. Playing bridge. Utterly pointless.

So… Jack of all trades, and master of none. Yes?

To some extent, I'd agree. Single-mindedness is one of the ingredients of success in any enterprise. Given a modicum of talent, it's probably the most important.

But you must remember that throughout my whole life, while I was enjoying these games...

Games? Didn't I take them seriously then?

Of course I took them seriously. Every one had the potential to change my life.

...while I was enjoying these games, running parallel I had my core obsession: storytelling in all its forms (books, theatre, film, television), and later the modern take on Buddhism. I have given official teaching on both these subjects.

What's more, such a wide area of general knowledge is a perfect hinterland for someone wanting to be a producer – especially the producer of *Doctor Who.* Though my prime interest was always in the artistic side of the job, I had enough knowledge in all the branches of production to be able to be an active collaborator with those on the other side of the ridiculous fence that has been erected between the two approaches, the artistic and the technical.

Three examples:

1. In one production – not a *Who* story, and it would be invidious to say which – we had cast an actress (I refuse to call her an actor) who was getting on for 30 to play a 17-year-old. Her face was perfect, but for the bags under her eyes.

   Now, the way to overcome this is simple. You just paint out the shadow cast by the sagging skin with a tone lighter than the general colour of the face. But you have to do it as a painter would. If you brush the highlight onto the cheek below the shadow as well, it serves to emphasise instead of hiding what you want to hide.

Yet this is what many junior make-up assistants do, remembering the rule but not understanding the purpose of the highlight.

I spotted this on our leading lady, and was able to point it out to our very busy make-up designer, who put it right at once.

2. Again, not Who. At the end of *Great Expectations*, the ever-popular Dickens story, the ancient wedding dress of the strange Miss Havisham catches fire from the candles, and the blaze kills her.

   Unfortunately, the cameras at Pebble Mill in Birmingham were not quite so up-to-date as those in London; and as Joan Hickson, who was playing the part, flailed about in terror, the flames dragged after them an ugly white irregular flare, which ruined the effect; and none of the technicians could think of anything to do about it.

   I suggested that they should use the peak white signal of the flare to key in a synthetic colour which matched the flame.

   They tried it, and it worked well enough to minimise the nastiness of the flare.

3. The one of which I'm most proud! Bernard Wilkie, the senior Visual Effects designer on *Planet of the Spiders* in 1974, was an old colleague. When I played my Arabian Nights prince on Boxing Day 20 years earlier, he and Jack Kine, who had by now become the head of the large and thriving Visual Effects, were the entire department. It was Bernard who put me on my flying carpet, and we'd often worked together since.

   So I felt that I could disagree with him when he told me that the best way to give our giant spiders life was as stationary rod puppets, and one mechanical one to run across the floor.

This sounded to me like a recipe for repeating the inadequacy of the dinosaurs we'd suffered at the beginning of the season (yes, I know I haven't told you about it yet. Anon, anon, good sir or madam).

I wanted a leading spider who could act. So I suggested a marionette, a stringed puppet.

'No, no,' said Bernard, 'you'd never get a natural action – and the strings would give the game away.'

I went home and brooded about it.

Now, I was at the time in the first throes of a love affair with CSO – Colour Separation Overlay, as the BBC dubbed it. The rest of the world calls it Chromakey. This is the 'blue screen process' that enables you to put an actor into any background you like. It was in its early stages, and we had had great fun on *Who* experimenting with it. I'll talk about it a bit more later. I suddenly realised that CSO could be the answer.

So, over the weekend, I dug out some wire coat hangers, the sort that you get from the dry cleaners, a load of corks (now where did they come from?) and, just using a pair of pliers from my toolbox, I made a jointed skeleton spider with a body about a foot long and legs to match. I then strung it in the traditional way one would use to string a horse (or Muffin the Mule – and how that dates me) but with twice as many legs; and I took it in on Monday. Bernard, who was a generous soul, was delighted with it, and called the other designers over to see it doing its tricks. He had one caveat.

'What about the strings?'

Aha!

'The spider can have its own little stage, with its own floor and a blue backing. We'll put it into the set using CSO. The strings will vanish into the blue.'

And so it turned out. I employed Barry Smith, one of the leading puppeteers in the country, to operate it, and Ysanne Churchman to voice it, and it gave a magnificent performance.

It wasn't only words that I didn't have to explain to Terrance. Though his reading was (and is) centred on classic thrillers (John Buchan; Dorothy Sayers; Margery Allingham; Raymond Chandler; Dashiell Hammett…) and superbly written modern historical novels (Patrick O'Brian; Dorothy Dunnett; Georgette Heyer…), it was (and is) so wide that any reference I made to an idea or a fact in practically any field was instantly picked up.

And vice versa.

Once we started talking, we couldn't stop. And we haven't stopped for the last 40 years.

We're both storytellers, fascinated by the craft; and we were both hellbent on curing the endemic malady of series television: late scripts – or, worse, no scripts at all.

That meant getting ahead of the game; and an active collaboration with the writers. Gone were the days when a storyline or a draft script would be tossed back with a few unhelpful notes.

The biggest thing that made a difference was entirely Terrance's: once we'd made up our mind to go with a particular idea, he would say to the writer, 'We're going to make this work. Between us we'll come out with a viable show.'

The knowledge (especially for writers new to the game or new to *Who*) that they were not on trial gave the whole enterprise an aura of confidence and trust.

The corollary of this was that I was always very much involved, right up to the point where we were happy with the scripts.

This can't be said about some producers, who just leave the whole job to the script editor; and then grumble if it doesn't pan out. And others, too much involved, keep changing their minds, coming up with so many 'improvements' that the original spark is lost.

This could all sound as if I wasn't happy to let Terrance play his role. On the contrary. I always say that the producer and the script editor should be a double-headed Beeblebrox; which is why I also tried to involve Terrance in as many production decisions as possible – which ultimately led to him taking over from me as the producer of the BBC1 Classic Serial 15 years later.

We had a very flexible routine on *Who*. (Depending on the writer, especially one of our regular stalwarts, some of the steps might be missed out.)

As with *Inferno*, the writer would come to us with a basic idea; or we would come up with one between us and ask a writer to have a go at it.

As it might be…

An eager young pup from the Midlands, Bill Shaxper by name, writes in with a corker of an idea.

It fits in with our plans, so Terrance and I discuss it, and then he asks young Bill to come in for a script conference with the two of us – a script conference which is very like a themed brainstorming session.

'The only snag that I can see now,' Terrance says, after a long and fruitful discussion, 'is that the old scientist hasn't got anybody to talk to. If he's stranded on this planet with only his robot and the monster, it's going to make his scenes very dull. Or is that why he's gone round the bend?'

'No, he only cracks up at the end,' says Bill. 'Why don't I give him a daughter? Call her… Miranda?'

'Better still,' say I, 'Make it a son – very young, little more than a teenager – and Jo Grant can fall in love with him.'

'Yes. That fits in well' says Bill.

He makes a couple of notes. Then he says in a working-it-out sort of a way:

'If Prosper's got a son… perhaps it would be better to make the scientist a woman. And the Doctor can fancy her…'

That notion is firmly stamped on, and Bill is sent away with enough material to write a fairly detailed storyline, which will then be discussed, analysed and developed in the same way at another script conference.

Once we're happy with the basic shape, I bow out for a while. Terrance then prises from poor Bill (and I speak advisedly, because this is where the hard work lies) a scene-by-scene breakdown showing exactly what happens in each episode.

Only when he's happy with this (and if he isn't he'll come up with suggestions to make it work, rather than just being negative) will he unleash the panting Shaxper and let him write the first draft.

Each episode, as it comes in, will be read by both Terrance and me, and any rewrites agreed.

And that's it. We just didn't have the time for the multiple rewrites that they go in for nowadays.

Come to think of it, it could make a good story, old Prosper on his planet, with his robot. Maybe the monster comes from his unconscious… *The Monster from the Id.*

Nah. It would never work.

A supreme example of Terrance's skill in sorting things out comes from this early period.

A script had been sent in to the BBC by a couple of aspiring young writers, Bob Baker and Dave Martin (from Bristol, not Stratford-upon-Avon) which sheerly by accident landed on Terrance's desk instead of with the intended Script Unit.

It was a comedy based on their experiences of National Service as reluctant squaddies. It was so good that Terrance asked me to read it and suggested that he should invite them in for a chat – during which they came up with a possible *Who* idea.

So he asked them to go away and expand it into a rough synopsis, which we could discuss. This was quite a usual step; a couple of pages of A4 could give you a pretty good taste.

A couple of pages of A4? What arrived was thicker than a couple of complete scripts put together.

It started with the crash landing in Hyde Park of an alien spaceship shaped like a giant human skull. Never mind, we could always move it to a deserted beach somewhere; and it didn't have to be a skull…

I read the first few pages with mounting enthusiasm. A hook that grabbed you and wouldn't let you go was followed by a string of surprises; original twists on old themes, and ideas out of the usual run.

But two or three pages later, I ground to a halt. I had to turn back to try and work out the run of the story; and the further I got into it the more confused I was. I never managed to get to the end.

To my relief, Terrance had had the same experience. Never mind the gigantic skull; the Bristol boys (as we were already calling them) had come up with a gargantuan Christmas pudding stuffed with far too much fruit.

It took Terrance nearly a year to tame them (now there's a succulent image: a couple of wild beasts slaving over a hot stove). Every time they had a go at following his suggestions, they came up with another cornucopia of inspiration.

Although they were gradually learning the necessary discipline it was beginning to seem that we'd go into production at the turn of the century. If we were lucky.

So, in the end, Terrance shut his office door, went into his editing mode for several hours, and emerged with a four-part scene-by-scene breakdown meticulously crafted from the several reams of paper in their file.

'Write that,' he told them firmly (but I'm sure in a kindly fashion).

The Claws of Axos was the very successful result – and the first of eight serials they were to give us and our successors between 1971 and 1979.

What's more, it was the Bristol Boys who came up with K9, the Doctor's robot dog.

What's more more: much later, Bob was the co-writer with Nick Park of the Oscar-winning *Wallace and Gromit* films from Aardman Animation.

All this thanks to the intensive lessons in story structure they'd had sitting at the feet of Professor Terrance Dicks.

And I'm only half joking. If at all.

CHAPTER 13

At first glance the idea of running a long-running series like *Who* might seem a simple task; difficult maybe, and hard work, but not complex; just a matter of doing each story in turn, after all.

Forget it.

In the first place, when you're in the thick of it, you, your script editor and your secretary, and more recently your production associate and location manager – the permanent team – could find themselves coping with three directors and their teams at the same time.

One is in the run-up period: casting the guest actors, having planning meetings, discussing and sorting out sets, costumes, monsters, visual effects, finding locations, going on recces, planning the camerawork, and so on, and so on.

The next is in the throes of production, either shooting the outside locations or on the studio turnaround – and you'll already have an idea how demanding that can be.

The third is wrestling with post-production: editing, working with the composer for the music cues (spotting them and recording them) and with Radiophonics for the rest of the sound effects, sound dubbing; and reviewing the finished article – which includes showing it to the Head of Serials for his final approval, which isn't always forthcoming.

And just to make things even more of a tangled web, these things can overlap even within the limits of one story. The film editing, for instance, will be started even during location filming, and probably won't be complete by the time you're in rehearsals for the studios.

You, the producer, if you're doing your job properly, have to find the balance between leaving everything to sort itself out (if you're lucky), having a creative input yourself, and being a control freak who never delegates.

You need to give everybody the freedom to do their job as part of the whole enterprise but at the same time steer everyone in the right direction, keeping as light a hand on the reins as possible.

You have to have no reluctance to intervene if it's necessary. I have known a director to misunderstand a script so radically that it would have made nonsense of the whole story if I hadn't twigged what was going on. And I came to a final run at the rehearsal room of one of the Classic Serials to find the leading actor giving a perfect imitation of Laurence Olivier's voice in *Richard III* – and neither he nor the director had noticed.

But above all, you have to be the Big Grandpa (the Director is Big Daddy or Mummy) to whom everybody looks for stability, inspiration, and help.

Quite a job.

So what's left?

The most important element of all. The scripts. Or have I said that before?

Ah, but maybe you haven't taken on board the sheer quantity of words that are going to be generated. As many as 26 25-minute episodes a year…

26 multiplied by 25 is 650; 650 divided by 90 is 7.22. So we have the equivalent of the scripts for seven feature films being discussed, storylined, written, delivered, rewritten during the year. The script editor is swimming

in paper, and the producer too is wading in the shallows most of the time.

And that's not even taking into account the tsunami on the horizon: the 11 hours, near as dammit, needed for next season.

Had any ideas arrived unsolicited? Who were we going to ask to have a go? Should we stay with the tried and true, or should we risk a newcomer?

Should we cover ourselves with an extra story in case the new bod delivered a turkey?

More to the point, what sort of stories did we want?

And so on and so on.

I feel an enormous sense of gratitude for the fact that Terrance and I hit it off. It must be hell for the producer and script editor who don't. You'd dread going to work.

So the main concern for Terrance and me in our discussions was the nitty-gritty of the current and the forthcoming seasons – the stories and the writers.

In between we ranged over a multitude of subjects, but many of them would be *Who* led.

We might, for instance, delve into the contradictions of cosmology.

Few people have a sense of how empty space is, or how large; and this means that you very quickly run into the mind-boggling contradictions of common sense which constitute the propositions of Relativity, and so you have to invent fantasy answers like the TARDIS's voyages through the 'Time Vortex', which is 'outside' our usual space-time continuum.

But even thinking of what time is in terms of time travel stories is like trying to pick up a handful of water. Our feeling that time is some sort of movement is built in to our language. We use expressions like 'time *passing*'; or 'I was enjoying myself so much that the afternoon *went by* in a flash'; and so on.

We have a mental picture of tomorrow morning coming towards us (and so it is in a sense, as the Earth turns and takes us towards the sunlight) or else we think of ourselves as moving through the events of our lives from the past to the future.

Either way, if time is moving, how fast is it going? (To say that its speed is subjective is not relevant to the question I'm asking.) You can't measure its speed with a speedometer in mph. Even to ask the question implies that there's another time beyond time, that you could measure its speed by. Let's call it meta-time. Perhaps our time goes by at one minute per meta-minute.

Great. That's that one sorted.

Hang on a moment. How fast does meta-time go? One meta-minute per meta-meta-minute? And meta-meta-time goes at one per meta-meta-metaminute?

And meta-meta-meta-time at… It's like the reflections of a candle put between parallel mirrors. There's an infinite number of flames. The mind goes into boggling mode, just as it does if you try to visualise the equivalent of a cube with an extra spatial dimension at a right angle to the other three.

So maybe our commonsense notion of the present moment carrying us from the past into the future is just an illusion. Maybe what we call time is nothing but our perception of the continually changing world.

But one thing is sure. For time travel stories we have to stay with our gut feeling, our intuition, however false it may be, that in some sense the whole of history, past, present and future, exists simultaneously, and that we can ride backwards and forwards on our time machine hopping on and off as we please.

And this brings us smack up against the paradoxes of travelling in time.

One of the things that Terrance and I agreed on from the start was that it was the utmost rubbish to say, as the first Doctor was apt to whenever he and his companions travelled into our past, 'We must be careful not to interfere with the course of history.'

And yet he cheerfully intervened when he was in our future, or on another planet.

Think about it. For a Time Lord travelling in a TARDIS the future and the past are defined by where you happen to be. Everything is history. History is what happens.

If you're going to be pernickety, the Doctor has no choice. His very presence will 'interfere with the course of history'. A time traveller inevitably becomes part of the inexorable sweep of multitudinous causes and effects that produce the moment in time where he ends up.

But perhaps his travelling takes the form of merely watching, observing. Even then, the very knowledge that he gleans from his jaunts will affect his present day when he returns. There's the other classical paradox, for instance: I go into the future. I see an invention, a 'Now, why didn't I think of that?' idea. I come back to my present, patent it and make my fortune. So who invented it?

We have to face it. It looks as if the only reality is the present moment. The past has gone and the future doesn't yet exist.

This means that travel into the past on a macro-level (i.e. leaving the weird world of the quantum out of it) is impossible. It would entail winding back the entropy of the entire universe. That's changing the course of history in spades.

And if you don't quite get what I'm on about, just try uncooking a pan of scrambled eggs, separating the whites from the yolks, fitting the right ones into the right shells, and shoving the completed eggs up the right hens' oviducts, ignoring their indignant back-to-front squawks.

Quite apart from whether it could be possible or not, the notion makes nonsense of all time travel stories.

This was one of my objections to the *Doctor Who* TV film (that indigestible mish-mash that wasted the talents of the excellent Paul McGann). We actually see the utter failure of the Doctor's endeavours and the beginning of the end of the world; and then…

Hey presto! Abracadabra!

With a wave of the scriptwriter's magic wand, time is reversed, and we have a happy ending. It's a cheat.

So did we never cheat?

Of course. Whenever any of us get embroiled in a time travel tale, we're all guilty of glossing over the logical difficulties, the possibilities of paradox.

I meant that the film cheated in storytelling terms. It just made the resolution too easy.

Here's another tip for all aspiring scriptwriters and producers. If you have an implausibility, something that doesn't quite make sense, have one of your characters point it out before the audience has a chance to notice.

The prime example of our doing this comes in *Day of the Daleks.*

The story is really a variant of the most famous time paradox of all: killing your granddad before he met grandma, for example, so your mum was never born. So how can you exist to kill granddad?

The story is of a group of guerillas from a future where the Daleks have taken over. They have travelled back with the intention of changing the course of history (with a bomb) so that their people will never be enslaved. But if they succeed, then they won't exist (in the future) as a resistance group, so how can it be that they have come back?

Curiously enough, these traditional paradoxes can be fairly simply argued away, by using one or other variant of the parallel world idea. We didn't try on this occasion, but Jo Grant was somewhat exercised about the whole concept.

She and the Doctor have been imprisoned by the guerillas, and in the Doctor's time-honoured expression, all they can do is wait.

Jo gets thinking.

'If these guerillas can travel back in time, and things go wrong for them,' she says, 'all they have to do is go back a day earlier, and this time get it right...'

Mm. If only the Doctor could get full control of the TARDIS, the same thing would apply to him. Bang goes the series, and we're all out of work.

But the Doctor says it's impossible.

'Why?' says Jo.

'Because of the Blinovitch limitation effect.'

'What's that?'

'Well, you see...'

Luckily, at that moment the door opens and in come their captors, so the Doctor can't explain any further. And he never gets round to it...

Come to think of it though, there could certainly be one big snag. If he did go back to have another go, there would now be two Doctors in one time, the one who got it wrong, and the one who's come back. And unless Doctor Two was able to have a word with his twin, which might prove impossible, Doctor One would unwittingly make the same mistake again, and come back again; and then there'd be three; with the ever present possibility of a non-stop proliferation of Doctors.

So it's just as well the Blinovitch limitation effect exists. I wish I knew what it is.

An example of another problem and a possible solution: The Doctor goes into the future on the May Bank Holiday Monday, after breakfast, leaving Jo Grant behind with the Brig at UNIT HQ. Right. He stays for a week, has a go at solving the problems there, and then pops back to pick up his sonic screwdriver, which he left on the mantelpiece.

Does he return on the Bank Holiday just in time for elevenses, which logically he could? No, when he comes back it's a week later.

Why?

Because we need it for the story, that's why. We need to be able to cut back to the Brigadier and Jo and see them in the present, coping with the exigencies of the plot while he's away.

How can you explain this?

You don't. You're left with no option but to ignore it.

But you need to know the shape of what you're doing, so that you don't run into any real faux pas; just as a writer or an actor will often know far more about a character's back story, as it's termed, than is revealed to the audience.

So what's the answer?

Aha! You don't start thinking like a Time Lord for nothing.

As taught at the Academy on Gallifrey in the second year: to travel in time in a linear fashion, as HG Wells's Time Traveller did, overtaking the unfolding events like a Ferrari with a vroom-vroom driver passing an old Austin Seven would need a phenomenal amount of energy.

But according to the textbook co-written by Professors Letts and Dicks, the students learn that the structure of time, luckily, is a multi-dimensional spiral – situated appropriately in the Time Vortex.

So a TARDIS going into the future can hop from one turn of the spiral to the next quite happily (and because it and the spiral are both multi-dimensional it can jump 20,000 years as easily as it can 20), but when it returns, say a week later, it finds itself a week later at home. Its departure position on the 'upper' turn of the spiral and its arrival position on the 'lower' have moved in parallel.

We might have rocketed the TARDIS between the turns of our helix through a wormhole. But wormholes hadn't been invented in the 1970s.

Talking of professors...

After we'd been going three or four years, I had a letter from a philosophy don at one of the newer universities, telling me that he was giving a talk on the possibility of time travel at a seminar of one of the philosophical societies, and had incorporated some of our ideas.

I wish I'd kept the letter. It was an improvement on the one I got from another PhD.

This one had nothing to do with time.

Like many a *Who* monster, the giant maggots in *The Green Death* which were causing all the grief were impervious to bullets.

The line I'd written for the Doctor was, 'Not a chance, Brigadier. Thick chitinous plates protecting the whole body surface. It's armour-plated.'

Jon, ever wary of scientific jargon, asked me how to pronounce 'chitinous'.

Off the top of my head I said, 'Oh, chit-inous. As you might say, "some chit of a girl"'; and then I forgot all about it.

Jon was right to be wary. Two days after the transmission I had the letter, which was short and to the point:

Dear Barry Letts,
The reason I'm writin'
is how to say kitin,
Yours sincerely...

CHAPTER 14

So there we were, with the go-ahead for the second season, and one story (possibly) in the pipeline – the one from the Bristol Boys. So how did our discussions go? Well, as I said for a start, we had to make up our minds about the sort we wanted.

We didn't even have to discuss the question of the seven-part serial.

We'd got away with *Inferno* – but only just.

Producing a seven-parter was like sprinting across a muddy field with gum-boots on. Never again!

Then again, the Doctor had been banished to Earth – ultimately to save money, as with the seven-parters. Although his exile had certain production advantages, as I've already said, we both felt it was a very severe constraint.

Mac Hulke, when he heard of the plans from Terrance, even before I joined, said, 'That means you've only got two plots: alien invasion and mad scientist.'

In spite of the ingenuity of the writers in finding variations on the theme, Jon's first year had already shown us four versions of the former.

The sixth floor of the Television Centre was where the Big Boys hung out. (NB No Big Girls like nowadays.) On the sixth floor the corridors were carpeted. On the sixth floor you had to have a key to the loo.

Every so often, producers, directors and editors from every corner of the Beeb would be invited to the sixth floor for a meeting (and later, dinner) with the bosses – Huw Weldon, David Attenborough, Paul Scott et al – to discuss future policy.

At one of these meetings, I heard a senior editor say… No, you're never going to believe it. I can hardly believe it myself. But it's true.

He was fearful of creeping tabloidisation of the Beeb's output of News and Current Affairs, saying that we should think of ourselves as the equivalent of the broadsheet papers.

He actually said, 'We mustn't be afraid of boring the viewer.'

I'm glad to say that he was shouted down (in a genteel Beebish way) by everyone there.

With this book comes a free gift; a gift that you will thank me for time and time again.

It's one of the most important tips you'll ever be given, whether you are a poet, a novelist, a musician, a painter, an architect (or any other sort of artist); a school teacher, a university lecturer, a vicar giving a sermon, a best man proposing the toast to the bride, a retiring chairman giving a thank you speech for his gold watch (or his £5m golden handshake), a football coach trying to save his team from relegation by a pep talk at half-time, the wit with a glass in his hand and a joke on his lips, a dog trainer; an actor (or actress!), a director, a set designer, a lighting cameraman, a choreographer… Have I missed anybody?

Oh yes, of course. A producer of *Doctor Who.*

How did a dog trainer get in there?

Pavlov, in his original experiments with dogs, discovered something surprising. A conditioned reflex eventually starts to weaken if it is consistently reinforced. To keep it strong you must occasionally miss out the conditioning stimulus.

Habituation has a physiological basis.

Okay, let's get less technical. What I'm saying is that the brain/body downplays any sensory information which is constant, or repetitive.

As I'm sitting here tapping away at my Mac, there's some sort of construction work going on not far away. A while ago, there was a loud bang. Not an explosion, but a big enough noise to catch my attention and make me go and look.

As I did so, there was another bang. And another.

Ah! A pile driver.

I came back to my desk and, for a time, each bang made me jump a little, and I couldn't get back into my stride; but within a few minutes I was back in my head, and the noise had receded so far into the background that I completely ceased to notice it.

Wait for it, wait for it. I'm sure you're getting the point, but I want to go into the matter a little more thoroughly just so you see how important it is.

Imagine that you're in the depths of the country, having a picnic. The blueness of the sky is as deep as the silence, which is broken only by the lazy hum of a bumblebee. All is still.

And then, far away across the fields, a tiny figure stands up beyond a hedge. Another picnicker? The farmer, having finished his lunch? Whatever.

Whoever.

The point is that your eye immediately flashes to the movement. And when you think that the stimulus on your retina must be in the order of a nanometre, your immediate reaction suddenly becomes extraordinary.

What's it all about?

It's a survival tactic. The jungle recedes into the background; but the stirring of some leaves, or an unusual noise, and the whole being is instantly alerted to the possibility of danger.

The cousins of your ancestors who lacked this faculty were eaten by lions, which severely limited their capacity to have descendants.

It's called natural selection.

If you bore your audience, you've lost them.

Now why couldn't I have just said that? Why go into all that malarkey about habituation?

Because it's a truism, a platitude, that's why. Something that's so accepted as true that it's no longer even worth saying it, because people just go 'Yeah, yeah. So what else is new?'

If you give the brain the same stimulus over and over, it literally switches off.

That's so important that I'll say it again.

If you give the brain the same stimulus over and over, ***IT LITERALLY SWITCHES OFF.***

The speaker/teacher/lecturer/actor who goes fast/slow; quiet/loud; high pitch/low pitch; solemn/jokey; pausing/running – not in an arbitrary way, but stemming from the content of what they are trying to get across – will be the one listened to. And that is the pattern for all the others in our list who are trying to grab their audience.

But the principle is far more than just a tool of the craftsman. I'd go so far as to assert that it contains the key to what is beautiful or significant in all the arts. In painting as in sculpture; in music as in poetry; the kernel of our perception is our awareness of similarities and differences, often at the same time.

Think, for example, of the rhymes, the assonances, and the metaphors of poetry, which bring them together. To stand and marvel at the subtlety of the tones on the skin of the Rokeby Venus is to see with Velasquez's eye the delicate differences, not apparent in even the best reproduction, which make the painting something quite other than a coloured photograph.

Gerard Manley Hopkins upped the thought into an appreciation of the beauty of creation:

Glory be to God for dappled things –
For skies of couple-colour as a brinded cow;
For rose-moles all in stipple upon trout that swim;
Fresh-firecoal chestnut-falls; finches' wings;
Landscape plotted and pieced – fold, fallow, and plough;
And all trades, their gear and tackle and trim.
All things counter, original, spare, strange;
Whatever is fickle, freckled, (who knows how?)
With swift, slow; sweet, sour; adazzle, dim;
He fathers forth whose beauty is past change:
Praise Him.

Variety, that's the secret.

You'd think this was obvious, but no. Take film and TV directing for example.

In my time I've seen many fashions come and go; and, in the desperate attempt of directors to escape from the established norms of screen grammar, and show their creative originality, they often violate the principle of variety.

What could be more understandable? But babies and bathwater come to mind.

To have nothing but beautifully composed wide shots was all the rage in the BBC plays department at one time, whereas during the same period some directors in series and serials felt that they were only up to the minute if some 90% of their shots were in big close-ups.

Perhaps the most usual mistake is the frenetic chasing of pace, especially in action movies. This can end up as the most irritatingly boring of the lot.

Quick unmotivated cutting with no apparent rationale behind it is the in thing at the moment. It'll pass, become old-fashioned, as yet new directors come up behind, just as the rediscovery of silence as a dramatic tool will sooner or later replace the current fad for music as wallpaper.

All these things have their place as part of the grammar of storytelling on the screen, of course. But the secret is how you use them.

The secret is VARIETY.

With this in mind, Terrance and I rapidly came to the conclusion in our deliberations that we must get the Doctor back on his travels as soon as possible.

We didn't want to lose the advantages of the UNIT set-up. But it musn't become boring.

We decided that we'd have at least one story where the Doctor and his companion were transported to an alien planet; so Mac Hulke was freed from the shackles he'd identified, and set about writing *Colony in Space,* which became the fourth story of the second season.

But how to inject a note of difference into the rest? And more to the point, what could we come up with for the opening show that would catch the attention of the great British public? Not to mention the editor of the *Radio Times*, who had the front cover in his gift.

When we are asked which of the two of us had a particular idea, Terrance and I are often at a loss. So many things just emerged from our wide-ranging discussions that it's often impossible to give an answer.

But we both have a very clear memory of the creation of the Master.

Several people had remarked on the similarity of the relationship of the Doctor and the Brigadier to that of Sherlock Holmes and Dr Watson; and out of this sprang the thought that what we needed was a Moriarty.

In a matter of minutes the character came alive. The point of Moriarty was that he was the great detective's equal; equal in intellect, equal in will, but as evil as Holmes was good.

What could the Doctor's enemy be but a renegade Time Lord?

So far so mutual.

But in the next instant, I said, 'And I know the very person to play it: Roger Delgado!'

Roger, who had run me through off the beach at St Leonards; Roger, who as the most sinister member of the Gestapo, chased me across the border into neutral Switzerland; Roger, the gentle soul who could freeze your blood with a look.

And the very next day, Terrance came in exultant. 'I've got the perfect name for him: the Master!'

Perfect indeed. Carrying on the academic overtones of the Doctor's own name; not only a Master of (evil) Arts, but having the authority of the Master of an ancient college.

We asked Bob Holmes to write our opening story, introducing the Master, and the result was *Terror of the Autons.*

The *RT* front cover was a masterpiece. An enormous close-up of Roger dominated it, with the figures of the Doctor and the Brig lurking in the background.

I was really chuffed.

Jon, however, was decidedly unchuffed.

'People keep asking me how I feel about Roger Delgado taking over as the Doctor,' he complained.

Despite what I said earlier, Jon could be very prickly, not to say petulant, if he felt that his position as Centre of the (*Who*) Universe was threatened.

All I could do was to apologise, and explain that it was the *Radio Times*'s design, not ours. I didn't tell him that I'd very happily approved it.

The story has a sequel.

Two years later, as a result of the yearly hunt for an intriguing gimmick, we relaxed our normally stringent fiat that the Doctor must never meet himself.

Time after time, both at home and at work, people had come up to us with the same suggestion, all convinced that they were the only ones to think of it.

'I've got a smashing idea,' they'd say. 'We've had three Doctors; why don't you have them meet each other?'

Well, yes. Come to think of it, it was a smashing idea. We should have listened to them earlier. So we asked the Bristol Boys to incorporate it in their next story, to be the season's opener with – keeping our fingers crossed – yet another front cover of the *Radio Times*.

What picture editor could resist?

So a photocall was arranged with Bill Hartnell, Patrick Troughton and Jon Pertwee. For some reason it was in a large private garage somewhere like Wandsworth, and I couldn't fit in an overseeing visit; so I asked Terrance to be my stand-in.

Terrance had a quiet but emphatic word with the photographer – and the resulting shot featured a very large figure, centre stage, with two much, much smaller portraits each side.

Guess who was in the middle.

CHAPTER 15

I haven't forgotten *Ambassadors of Death.* It was part of my exponentially steep learning curve, so I'm not likely to forget it.

Mike Ferguson was the director. One of the best.

One of the best. Now, that's an expression which has slipped out of use. It means 'a good egg' in the PG Wodehousian sense.

Well, so he was. He had a Bedford camping van, or motor caravan, which was dear to his heart; and he lent it to me to take my family to Cornwall.

A very good egg.

But that's not what I meant. I meant that he was one of the best directors, one of the most imaginative and creative, we had on *Who.*

That was the trouble.

The army was very much involved in *Ambassadors of Death,* especially the UNIT troops under the command of Brigadier Alistair Lethbridge-Stewart. Mike suggested to me that if we used the stunt group named Havoc recently set up by the stuntman and fight-arranger Derek Ware (a *Who* veteran since the very earliest times), rather than an ad hoc bunch of crowd artists, we'd not only have Derek's own expertise in the fight scenes, but a squad of trained men who knew how to handle guns, who could die in various spectacular ways.

Stuntmen are always eager to display their skill in the martial arts, both Eastern and Western, rather as Visual

Effects, usually the kindest and gentlest of boffins, love setting buildings on fire and are mad about blowing things up.

So it was obviously a good suggestion of Mike's.

Talking about Visual Effects and explosions, we had a battle at the end of *Terror of the Autons*, with Havoc stuntmen being blown up and literally flying through the air (via mini-trampolines).

At the end of the long hard day's filming, I was sitting in my car, feeling pretty shattered, and going through the shooting script for the next day. Everybody else had gone home.

Or so I thought.

A sudden face appeared at the window and I recognised a beaming Michealjohn Harris, our Visual Effects designer.

'Would you like to see a big bang ?'

Why not?

We'd finished all the battle stuff. From long experience, Michael had made sure that we'd have enough explosive to cover any eventuality – which meant a large quantity being left over; and according to the regulations he couldn't take it back to the Beeb.

So he'd stacked the lot into a pile in the middle of the field where we'd been shooting, and wired it up so that he could detonate it from the edge, just as if it were a bona fide special effect.

'Stand by,' he said.

All according to the usual routine.

It didn't go bang, it went WHOOMPH!!!

Michealjohn had included all the surplus smoke bombs in the mix so, apart from the earsplitting noise, a cloud of smoke billowed up with the mushroom shape of a mini atomic bomb going off.

Quite true.

'Good, eh?' said Michealjohn, with a grin of sheer delight.

Bonkers, the lot of them.

The trouble with Mike's suggestion about Havoc was that it was much more expensive; and I didn't think of that until later. But that's not all. He had another packet of goodies up his sleeve.

A hijacking. The baddies are after the three astronauts who have just returned to Earth.

Well, they would be, wouldn't they? It's the sort of thing that *Who* baddies get up to, especially if they can pull it off using nothing but a fake road sign and a couple of heavies with guns, as suggested in the script.

'Bit dull, isn't it?' said Mike.

'What do you suggest?'

'Mmm. I'll have a think.'

And he thought to the extent of a good dollop of Havoc, half a dozen motor bikes, a smoke bomb or two and…

'Of course, what would really make the sequence would be a helicopter.'

Of course. Why didn't that occur to me?

When you add the resulting bulge in the budget, which came near to bursting it, to the overruns in the studios, with Mike regularly having to ask for an extension to 10.30, you can understand why, in the end, I found myself having a bit of a chat with him. I wasn't trying to pull rank or exert my statutory authority (I'd already formulated my 'first among equals' doctrine, but just to myself; I hadn't yet pronounced it *ex cathedra*). After all, I had said yes to everything that he asked for.

'It's my job to push the system as far as it will go,' he said, 'and it's your job to tell me to stop.'

He was right of course. In every respect, it's the job of both the TV director *and* the producer to stretch the system to its limits, *and just a little bit over*. To go further is to steal resources from other programmes; to do less is not only to risk having your budget cut next time, but more importantly losing the extra zing that takes a show out of the 'good enough' category.

But it's obviously up to the producer to be the one to keep an eye on the larger picture.

As time went by I learnt to play the game that most producers do. That is to supply the director and his team with a detailed budget, in advance, but one which is not quite as large as the one locked away in the drawer. The difference can be reluctantly doled out when it becomes needed – as it certainly will, largely because the director knows the contingency fund exists!

There were other tricks we got up to. For a while, the BBC accountants played with an idea which was an early version of John Birt's hated Producer's Choice.

The new way of budgeting abandoned the concept of above and below the line costs – that is, real cash (above the line) which would be used to hire actors and so on and had to be rigidly stuck to, as opposed to the arbitrary and imagined costs (below the line) allocated to such things as studios and the time of staff members, which were granted without question, on the principle that the resources were there anyway and didn't have to be bought in.

Realising that the use of resources was out of control, they introduced 'Total Costing'. Resources were given a real cash value in the budget, which had to be adhered to. And as a sop to soothe the indignant producers (the system meant far more work), they made the below-the line-costs convertible into real cash if necessary.

That's where it went wrong.

The canny producer soon realised that he could, for example, put into his budget estimate a few days' filming at Ealing Studios, which were nominally expensive to hire.

Then, after it had been accepted, he would find to his surprise that the script didn't demand any studio pre-filming after all. The mythical studio rental could be converted into lovely lolly, which would buy a more prestigious star, or lusher costumes.

You can't trust anybody, can you?

Mike Ferguson was the person who got me fascinated by Colour Separation Overlay (CSO), or Chromakey.

Warning! The next chunk is for those with a geekish tendency like me who find all this stuff fascinating.

The technical backroom boys had been licking their lips like dogs waiting for a biscuit. When colour cameras arrived at the BBC, they were at last able to have a go at the process they had devised which was their electronic version of the 'travelling matte' used in films for such effects as the airborne Mary Poppins. This is also called the 'blue screen' process, though, just to make things awkward, Julie Andrews stood in front of a yellow screen; and nowadays the preference is for green, which couldn't be used in the early days because of the amount of green there is in our flesh colour.

So how does it work?

I've already talked about the matte, or mask, used in front of the camera to let us film a duplicate Pat Troughton in Enemy of the World. *A similar method could be used to mask a portion of a (static) shot, so that the set could be extended by a painting.*

For instance, you could have a very wide shot of your heroes standing at an impressive door which you had built in the studio, with the rest of the massive temple above their heads being the product of a scenic artist. It was a less time-consuming cousin of the well-known glass shot. The only snag was that the actors had to stay below the matte line, or their heads would vanish.

With the advent of colour, this disadvantage vanished. With travelling matte, the actors perform in front of a blue screen, the blue colour being a very intense, saturated spectral hue.

The resulting film is then twice rephotographed in the optical printer, once with a blue printing light, and once with a red/green light.

This gives you two strips of film: one which is so over exposed wherever the printer 'sees' blue that it is solid black, and so underexposed where the actors were that it is clear; and a second print which reverses this. You end up with two masks, to print first the actors and then the background.

The advantage, of course, is that the actors act as their own 'mattes', masking the background with their own bodies as they move around; hence the expression 'travelling matte'.

Colour Separation Overlay, or CSO (which the rest of the world calls Chromakey) is the electronic equivalent. How it differs from travelling matte in the technical details is another story. The principle is the same, and the result is the same.

Okay! The rest of you can come back now.

CSO meant that you could put an actor into any background. Mike and I persuaded the bosses to give us a couple of experimental studio days, one before *Ambassadors of Death*, and another before *Claws of Axos*, his next show, where we played around with different ideas.

For instance, Visual Effects brought down a model house; and with one camera on the house and the other on our AFM (assistant floor manager), Margot Heyhoe, coming round a blue flat and disappearing behind another, we had her appear round the corner and go through the front door. It almost worked, but the primitive apparatus couldn't yet reproduce the shadow of the actor.

This, combined with the high key lighting necessary to make it operate was apt to give the look of a cartoon character – and one floating in the air, unlike Mickey Mouse, who from the earliest days always had a shadow to anchor him to the ground.

Nevertheless, it was so useful a tool that we often used it during the next five years, sometimes with great effect, and sometimes ... ugh!

For example, we used it successfully in *The Green Death* to put our rod-puppet three-foot maggots into the studio sets; but the shot of the Doctor and Jo punting themselves through the mine in a coal truck, with real maggots in the model background, was just about the worst special effect we ever did – apart, of course, from those bloody dinosaurs in *Invasion of the Dinosaurs.*

The biggest trouble was that the signals from the two cameras often didn't quite synchronise, and the result was a horrid blue line outlining the character in the foreground. And the extent of it seemed to be quite unpredictable.

It seemed that it depended on the electronic weather.

Mitch Mitchell and Dave Jervis. These were the two, starting as junior cameramen delegated to do this lowly job of Video Effects, who became the acknowledged experts. They were both touched with a sort of genius.

I remember Mitch, who was officially on leave, coming in to see how his novice stand-in was getting on.

Not well.

There was a very thick blue line all the way down one side of the actor, and when the operator tried to tune it out, it jumped to the other side. It was completely unacceptable, and the Technical Manager was in despair.

'Mmm,' said Mitch. 'Give me 15 minutes, and I think I can fix it.'

He disappeared into the backroom, where all the electronic gubbins lived, and we got on with something else.

The Television Theatre, which used to be the Shepherd's Bush Empire, was where popular programmes were put on when a large live audience was part of the show. It was about half a mile away from the Television Centre on Shepherd's Bush Green.

I'm not changing the subject.

Mitch came back. 'Try it now,' he said.

It was perfect. The blue line had vanished utterly.

'It was a timing error,' said Mitch. (Don't ask me.) 'I routed one of the signals down to the Television Theatre and back, and that delayed it just enough to match it to the other signal. Simple.'

Einstein thought the Special Theory of Relativity was simple.

CHAPTER 16

From my first viewings of *Spearhead from Space* and *The Silurians* I had a couple of things I wanted to change.

One was the Doctor's assistant, Liz Shaw, played by Caroline John.

Now, I want to make it absolutely clear that I didn't lose the character because I thought Carry wasn't up to it. On the contrary, she's an outstanding actress. We later cast her in a leading part in *The Hound of the Baskervilles,* when Tom Baker played Sherlock Holmes.

The trouble was the concept of the clever scientist.

It seemed to me that, apart from screaming at monsters and having to be rescued, the companion had two functions: one, to give the pre-pubescent male viewer – and his elder brother (we'll leave Dad out of it) – a reason to rush home from the Saturday afternoon football match; and two, to ask the Doctor questions such as, 'What's going on?' or 'I don't get it. What does that mean?' so that he can not only explain to her, but also to the viewer.

The trouble with Liz Shaw was that she already knew all the answers; and as for the first requirement, the buzz around the office was that the photograph that got her the job (in addition, of course, to her acting ability) was one of Carry in a bikini.

And Liz Shaw was a fashionable young lady in a miniskirt.

But that did nothing to solve the problem of her being such a cleverclogs.

So now I had two difficult jobs: telling her that I wouldn't be asking her back for the next season, and finding a new companion.

At a *Who* convention a few years ago, I was sharing a panel with Carry, and I was shocked to hear her tell the audience that I gave her the news that we wouldn't be asking her back for the next season in her dressing room just before an evening recording.

I offered her a belated apology, there and then. I find it difficult to believe that I could have done such a crass, insensitive thing. I'd had enough experience of 'first night nerves' myself, for God's sake. I can only suppose that my head was too full of my new responsibilities.

As it happens, Carry would have turned down another contract anyway, because she was pregnant.

After Jo Grant, the replacement for Liz Shaw, hatched between Terrance and me, had appeared in the first serial of the new season, I had an indignant letter from a scientist who was a keen follower, not to say fan, objecting to the change; telling me off in very fierce terms, saying that, as UNIT's scientific adviser, the Doctor would have a fully qualified assistant.

I replied at once, saying that it was quite deliberate, enclosing the pages of the script that had the following dialogue:

```
THE DOCTOR HAS COMPLAINED TO JO GRANT THAT
SHE ISN'T A SCIENTIST.

JO: I took science at A-level...

THE DOCTOR IS NOT IMPRESSED. HE LATER BRINGS
UP JO'S APPOINTMENT WITH THE BRIGADIER.

BRIGADIER: You've been saying you needed a
new assistant ever since Miss Shaw went back
to Cambridge.
```

DOCTOR: Yes, but I need somebody as qualified as she was.

BRIGADIER: Nonsense, Doctor. As Miss Shaw said herself, you need somebody to hold your test-tubes and tell you how brilliant you are.

LATER:

DOCTOR: I thought you said you'd taken science.

JO: I didn't say I passed!

I then explained to our correspondent why I'd made the change.

She was gracious enough to write back and apologise.

While Jo wasn't just a screamer (she could do things on her own initiative, though they frequently went wrong), the actress had to be able to show us how scared she was. Obviously, she had to be attractive (am I being sexist here? No, just pragmatic). And she had to be able to take direction and work with the team.

So how did I set about finding Jo?

I set up a process which turned out to be so successful that I used the same method when I cast Jo's successor, Sarah Jane Smith.

It soon spread amongst the possible candidates and their agents that I was on the hunt; and from the multitude of suggestions I picked out those I wanted to meet.

All in all, during the two batches of interviews I saw nearly 200 girls, some of them for both parts.

I saw big ones, small ones, loud ones, quiet ones, dark ones, blonde ones… But they had one thing in common. They were all fiendishly attractive in their different ways; and most of them spilling over with personality. With a few that could have a double meaning, I must admit.

I can't remember on which occasion it was, the first or the second, but Jon took a keen interest in what I was doing, and suggested two candidates he'd met socially.

Terrance and I had a trip down to the rep in Westcliff-on-Sea – next door to Southend – to see the first, in a comedy by William Douglas Home, *The Amorous Prawn.* As far as I could judge anybody in such a weak play, she was a good actress; she was certainly beautiful and had a warm personality. But she was too tall and voluptuous. The relationship with the Doctor might have developed in quite the wrong direction!

Her name was Rula Lenska.

I turned down Jon's second choice using similar criteria. To call her striking would be like calling a man-eating lioness cute.

Michael Caine obviously thought so too. Her name was Shakira Baksh and he married her.

I didn't ask any of those who I asked to come in to meet me to read for me, as was the norm, and I tried to make the extended interview – at least 45 minutes – as friendly and chatty as possible. I'd had some nasties myself, and I was determined never to subject anybody to the same humiliation.

I once had a well-known theatre director say to me, 'Come now, Mr Letts. I'm sure you can do better than that. Try again.'

That's what I call really helpful direction. I should have walked out, but I was desperate. PS: I didn't get the part.

And a Scouse director of TV commercials, casting a milkman, said to me with a sneer (a real visible one), 'And what sort of northern accent do you call that?'

It was an absolutely authentic York accent. I'd been in the rep at the Theatre Royal twice, for a total of four years.

I still feel angry, on my own behalf, and on behalf of all the poor blighters who are still going through it.

For the auditions, I'd written a short two-handed scene with a black magic theme. (It was Terrance who later suggested that I should expand it into a full length story, *The Daemons*.)

I wanted to cast the new character, Captain Mike Yates, at the same time; and I already had two prime candidates, Ian Marter and Richard Franklin, two very different types, either of whom could have played Mike, so I employed them in turn to be the other half of the two-hander with Jo. In the event, it turned out that Ian wasn't available for a long contract, so I never had to make the choice – and Ian joined us later, first in *Carnival of Monsters*, and then as Doctor Harry Sullivan, one of the companions with Tom Baker.

If I thought she was a possible I gave each Jo a copy of the script, and asked her to learn it as if she were going to play it for real.

Once I'd whittled the list down, I took a proper rehearsal room at the 'Acton Hilton' (not a five-star hotel, just the BBC rehearsal block), and employed an assistant floor manager to mark out the limits of the imaginary set, just as we would for a real rehearsal.

And then, over a couple of days, I worked with each actress in turn for a couple of hours. We blocked the scene for moves and imaginary cameras, we discussed it and worked on it as actors like (and need). We had a 'dress rehearsal', and then, after a coffee break, I would say, 'Okay, this is the performance. Give it all you've got.'

This way I really got to know each one of them and soon found out if (a) she really was an actress; (b) she could take direction; (c) she was pleasant to work with; (d) …now what was d?

Oh yes! If she could scream.

You'd think anybody would if they came face to face with the Devil.

But two of them couldn't.

It was a couple of days before we were going into the rehearsal room, and I'd completed my short list, when an agent rang me with the name of another girl.

She nearly lost the chance because she went to the wrong building. She was scatty; so short-sighted as to be almost blind; so tiny that two-shots with Jon would exercise all a director's skill; had enormous rings on all eight fingers; couldn't stop talking (she still can't); and was completely enchanting.

There was one slot left in the rehearsal room schedule.

If she could act as well – and if she could scream…

Her name was Katy Manning.

That first year was a busy one. (Come to think of it, all five were.) Not only did I have *Snowy Black* to sort out, and Don Houghton's writing of *Inferno*, and planning the next season, but I also had to take over the directing of *Inferno* from Dougie Camfield.

Douglas Camfield was one of the two directors (the other one being Christopher Barry) who had had most to do with *Who* since 1963 when it went on air the day after the assassination of President Kennedy. Dougie had been the production manager on the very first, and gone on to direct six of the most striking black and white *Who* stories. So I was very glad that he was available to direct *Inferno*.

I was very pleased when the new series of *Doctor Who* came out to see that one of the directors was my old friend and colleague, Graeme Harper.

Graeme Harper was my production manager when I was directing one of the classic serials. He was desperate to move on to directing; and we were discussing this during a lunch break.

'What depresses me,' he said, 'is that it seems that the only way to get on in this business is to be ruthless.'

Ruthless was the last word you'd use to describe the effervescent and sometimes too warm-hearted Graeme. (I'd had to move in and sack an inefficient and unhygienic location-catering firm for him.)

'In my experience,' I said, 'ruthlessness is a poor substitute for enthusiasm.'

It was as if I'd told him he'd won a holiday in the sun.

'I never thought of that,' he said. 'Thank you.'

Dougie Camfield was a perfect example of what I said to Graeme; he was the epitome of infectious enthusiasm. My most vivid memory of Dougie was in his office at an early planning meeting when he was trying to describe to the camera team a particular effect he was after.

He suddenly seized the waste paper basket and leapt onto the desk. He was a camera crane, and zoomed down from ceiling height, corkscrewing the camera (the basket) down to a close shot of the invisible primord (the *Inferno* monster) lying on the floor, which he could clearly see.

He not only worked out all his shots with that sort of precision, but his schedules would have not disgraced a Staff Major responsible for planning the retaking of Burma in WWII:

```
At 1427 we shall move to location D, being
set up by 1517 when we shall shoot scenes 5,
15, and 23. This will take 52 minutes.

Moving to location E at 1609...
```

Etc.

Maybe a bit of an exaggeration; but it wasn't surprising. He'd become an army officer when he did his

National Service, and he loved it. He always said that the biggest disappointment of his life was that he wasn't accepted into the SAS.

It was probably only because of marrying the actress Sheila Dunn and having a son that he didn't go off and join the French Foreign Legion – which became his passion and obsession. He wrote a *Who* script based on it and tried in vain to persuade my successor, Philip Hinchcliffe, to produce it.

A while after I'd left *Who,* when I was producing the BBC1 Classic Serial, I asked him to direct *Beau Geste,* our dramatisation of the archetypal Foreigh Legion tale. Paul Joel, the designer, created a legionnaires' fort in our Dorset desert which was so authentic, inside and out, that you had to give the walls a thump to prove to yourself that they weren't made of stone. We took an enormous risk, shooting the whole thing in a disused sand-quarry which went on for well over a mile, but we had glorious weather, and were rained off on only one day.

Dougie went to France to do preliminary research at his own expense; he employed an ex-sergeant to teach our actors the right drill (in the car park of the Acton Hilton); and he introduced a multitude of authentic touches to the script. His enthusiasm resulted in what I can only describe as the definitive version of *Beau Geste.*

But Dougie had a secret.

The film sequences on *Inferno* were all that I expected, including a spectacular fall by one of our Havoc team – one of the highest yet seen on British television.

Dougie then plunged straight into the rehearsals for the studios.

I'm not sure exactly when I had the phone call. My memory is that it was during the first week of rehearsals, but I've been told that it was three weeks into the seven-week stand.

It was Jon Pertwee himself on the other end of the phone. The production manager wouldn't have been there, and the AFM would be too involved to break away.

'Barry,' said Jon, 'I think you'd better come down. Dougie's not at all well. He's as white as a sheet and he can hardly stand, but he insists on going on.'

I went straight along. We put Dougie in a taxi, and Sheila, who was in the show, took him straight to hospital where he was admitted and stayed for a long time.

I took over as director for the rest of the serial, though we kept his name on it for a very good reason. He had a type of cardiac arrhythmia, tachycardia, a fluttering of the heart that lowers the blood pressure catastrophically.

He'd kept it secret, he told me later, because he was afraid he'd stop being offered work; and as a freelance that could have been calamitous. I promised to keep quiet.

I visited him in hospital, of course, but the next time that I saw him outside was at the party we had after the last recording.

'You know, Dougie,' I said, perhaps a bit pompously, 'television is nothing more than a very important game. It's important because it can affect people's lives, but it's not worth risking your own life for.'

He was appalled.

'I could never believe that I was devoting my whole life to a game!' he said.

He was now on a new drug regime which kept his dicky heart more or less under control – and confidential – for more than 13 years.

Beau Geste was such a success, both critically and in the ratings – and I thought it such a cracking good bit of direction – that I asked him to take on another of his favourite stories, the swashbuckling tale of Ruritania, *The Prisoner of Zenda.*

His official joining date as director was Monday 30 January 1984. Three days before, on the Friday, he went to bed early, feeling tired.

He fell asleep and never woke up.

I was far more concerned about his death on a personal level than professionally.

Luckily Leonard Lewis, most well-known for being the producer of *Softly Softly* for many years, had returned to directing, and the show went ahead as planned.

But I knew that Sheila, quite apart from her dreadful loss, would be in a hole. Working on *Prisoner of Zenda* would have paid the bills for quite a while; and suddenly there would be no money coming in.

So I went to Graeme MacDonald, my boss as the Head of Drama Serials, and asked him if the BBC could pay her something.

'How much would he have earned?' he asked. Leaving out such things as extra payments for the odd day's additional editing, the answer was £12,000 ($24,000). In today's money that would be something in the region of £30,000 ($60,000).

'Leave it with me,' said Graeme. 'I'll see what I can do.'

A little while after the funeral, Sheila arranged a memorial service for Dougie. They were both devout Christians.

All Souls in Langham Place, just down the road from Broadcasting House, was packed with BBC friends and colleagues. Graeme met me on the steps.

'I think you should be the one to give this to Sheila,' he said.

It was a cheque for £12000.

CHAPTER 17

My unaccustomed financial virtue in analysing the budget, my delving into the mysteries of the computer printout, produced some buried treasure: the programme had, without fail, always overspent on such things as visual effects and costume.

It seemed ridiculous that what was an inevitable cost wasn't paid for up front. I used this – and the unquestioned success of the first Pertwee season – to persuade the bosses to give us more money. All in all, we got enough together to escape from the dreaded monster, the seven-parter.

We were helped in this by Ronnie Marsh, who had emigrated from the Light Entertainment Department bringing the police series starring Jack Warner, *Dixon of Dock Green*, with him.

Ronnie backed us in our plans to increase the number of stories in each six-month season. He loved the idea of the 'first night' – a new beginning, with a chance to snag a new audience. And we started with a bang, asking Bob Holmes to reprise his idea of the Nestenes in *Spearhead from Space*, taking over a factory to create inimical living plastic with a mind of its own, a mind seemingly intent on destroying humans.

But of course, on this occasion the mind behind the mind behind the terror was that of our new villain, the Master! His precise intention was never made quite clear perhaps; this was nothing but a trial run of his attempt to control the Nestenes, but it's safe to assume that his ultimate motivation was a desire to dominate the entire planet.

Luckily, he didn't succeed on this occasion, or it would have meant not only the end of the Doctor's adventures but the end of my job as producer. But he certainly caused me enough trouble.

WHY MY CHILDREN WILL NEVER WATCH DOCTOR WHO AGAIN!

This was the banner headline over an article on the central leader page of the *Daily Express*, at that time the daily that claimed the largest circulation in the United Kingdom. The writer objected to such delights as the plastic blow-up chair which smothered the works manager of the factory for having dared to oppose the Master; and she didn't much fancy the telephone cord which tried to strangle the Doctor; or the plastic daffodils which spat out a killing spray.

I had a letter from a viewer complaining that, after seeing our plastic troll doll strangling the owner of the factory, her little boy was frightened to take his teddy bear to bed with him.

And after the episode where the Doctor pulled off the utterly convincing mask of a policeman to reveal the fearsome blank face of an Auton, I had a letter from the office of the Commissioner of the Metropolitan Police at New Scotland Yard pointing out that we were undoing all their efforts to get children to trust the police, and asking us (very politely) not to do it again.

I have heard it said that there were questions asked in Parliament. I can't vouch for that but, as Terrance always says, why let the truth get in the way of a good story?

The upshot of it all was a memo from MD Tel. This was the usual way of referring to the being who was one step away from being God. It stood for Managing Director, Television, God of course being known as the DG – the Director General. Along with the rest of the BBC we didn't really believe in the Governors, being convinced that they were metaphysical beings who didn't really exist.

MD Tel at this time was Huw Weldon. On one occasion, on a state visit to the Drama Serials Department, he had said that there were two BBC programmes that were a must in his household: football's *Match of the Day* and *Doctor Who.* But now, in the veiled terms of such missives, we were gently told that he would be keeping an official eye on the programme as well.

So Terrance and I decided that in future (to use Jon Pertwee's favourite image) we'd keep our Yetis (and their ilk) out of the bathroom and put them, if not into the Himalayas or the Underground, into Outer Space or such, where their scariness could be safely enjoyed.

But where there's Yin there's bound to be a spot of Yang lurking about. The curse of the seven-parter had meant that the ratings over the previous season had sunk from a very healthy 8.4 million for the first Pertwee episode to a worrying 5.5 for the last part of *Inferno.*

What's more, our position in the chart of the 200 top BBC programmes had sunk from 54 to 79.

Terror of the Autons not only whipped us back to 8.4 million, but pulled us up the list again to 59th place, a trend which continued throughout the season to the end, so that the last episode of *The Daemons* climbed to 17th.

And I'd bet Mrs Daily Express didn't get away with her threat. If I know anything about family life, her bairns would soon have been back in their rightful place behind the sofa.

Whenever the BBC takes a step in this direction – such as cancelling the first showing of Peter Watkins's

The War Game, the early drama-doc about the result of a nuclear attack; or banning Dennis Potter's play *Brimstone and Treacle*, which featured the rape of a disabled woman by a disguised Devil – they are accused of censorship. 'What about freedom of speech?' cry their critics.

I think this is nonsense. The BBC is in effect a publishing company, and as such must be an editor. You can always argue that a particular decision was wrongly made – I myself had a small hand in getting *The War Game* its belated showing, 20 years on – but to give a contributor the absolute right to put anything he liked on the screen would be to abrogate the Corporation's responsibility to their audience.

Terror of the Autons was the first Pertwee *Who* I directed myself… As I told you, the roast chicken of acting in the theatre was complemented by the chocolate mousse of television.

Producing and directing each have their own different rewards as well. Producing – at least the sort of creative producing I was lucky enough to be able to concentrate on – can become as satisfying as our regular Sunday dinners used to be: roast lamb with mint sauce; a joint of beef with Yorkshire pud; or yes, a plump capon with bread sauce; always different, but reliably and comfortably filling the tummy.

But producing, even at its best, can't compare with the joy of directing (when everything goes right!) – like the hit on a chocoholic's tongue of the first quarter teaspoonful of a *pot au chocolat.*

When it does all go well you feel as high as a kite. I remember arriving home on one such occasion and deciding that I was still far too full of energy to go to bed (and too full of Guinness too – and I'd just driven 12 miles back from the TV Centre. Stupid).

Everybody at home, and apparently everybody in the whole of Finchley, was fast asleep; so I went for a walk round the block – about a mile, I suppose. I still felt that I could jump over a mountain, but in lieu I decided to dance along a low brick wall in front of a garden. Halfway along I came to the gap at the front path.

Well, what would you do?

Yes, that's right. A graceful Nureyev-type leap took me soaring across to the other side, where I missed my footing and crashed down.

Luckily the doctor in Casualty must have had pretensions as a plastic surgeon. The minute stitches that fastened the flap of skin back onto my chin left only the faintest scar.

Filming at Robert Brothers Circus. I'd already been to a performance, and a terrific show it was too. The lady who sold the tickets turned out to be the lady with the ice cream tray at the interval, but nobody would have guessed that she was also the glamorous Madame Loulou who had the troupe of performing poodles.

She had another role into the bargain, as I found out the next day when I visited Bobby Roberts in his immense trailer van with the chromium-plated cocktail bar, and he introduced me to his wife.

I might have been quite envious. Being backstage in a circus must be even more addictive than working in theatre or television. But right now I had the best job in the world as director, and I dived in and let it sweep me along as if I were shooting the rapids; white-water rafting without a raft.

I told you that there was something else that I wanted to change. That was the extraordinary get-up they'd dressed the Brig in.

I felt strongly that unless the characters in *Doctor Who* were absolutely believable, especially in the way they dressed, it could easily degenerate into a theatrical gallimaufry (hey! what about that for a word!) a couple of gags away from a pantomime, or a musical comedy. As indeed it did at times in its later incarnations.

Nick looked as if he were about to burst into a song and dance routine, using his swagger cane as Fred Astaire used his walking stick.

As with the recasting of the companion, I felt the time to upgrade the uniform would be at the beginning of the second season, making the change less noticeable.

I rang up the Ministry of Defence and explained my problem: 'If there were such a thing as the United Nations Intelligence Task Force, what sort of uniforms would they wear?'

Their reaction wasn't quite what I expected.

'I say, are you responsible for that Brigadier character? You've got him spot on. We've any amount of them round here just like him!'

Well done, Nick. Well done indeed.

But it didn't answer my question.

'Oh, sorry. Well they'd all wear their usual uniforms, with United Nations flashes on their shoulders, and light blue berets with a UN badge.'

Ah… If they wore blue berets, even light blue ones, the top of their heads would vanish into a CSO background. In any case, we wouldn't want them to look like a peace-keeping force, would we? Might give entirely the wrong impression of who would be in power in the near future – which, at the time, I hoped would be the Liberal Party.

Which is why, a couple of years later, in *The Green Death*, a minister in a Cabinet meeting addresses the unseen prime minister as Jeremy, Jeremy Thorpe being the leader of the Liberals at the time.

Talking of which, in the same story, my co-writer, Bob Sloman, who had a wicked sense of humour, gave our villain, Stevens, the first name of Jocelyn, the name of his boss at the *Sunday Times*. We were lucky not to get a libel writ.

So I rang one of the top military tailors and asked them how much a Brig's uniform would cost me.

'£80 ($160),' they said.

'Done,' I said, 'I'll send him along.'

Recently I called another leading tailor (the first having merged with somebody) and asked him how much the same uniform would cost today. But I didn't get the same answer.

'£985 ($1970).' Cheap at the price.

So the Brig turned up at the circus in all his glory. Nick was obviously designed by nature to be a senior officer. Very unperceptive of the army, when he did his National Service, to overlook his potential. He was a trooper, the equivalent of a private.

Our UNIT team was now swelled by one. Captain Yates joined Sergeant Benton on the Brigadier's staff.

Richard Franklin, as bouncy as a new puppy (or as a young actor who's just starting a smashing job), appeared in front of me in his Captain's uniform, as I was waiting for the elephants to get into position.

'Haircut okay?' he said, beaming.

His hair at the back hung down from under his cap. If it hadn't curled under, it would have come over his collar. I'm sorry to say I laughed. I honestly thought he was joking.

You have to understand that since the years of Beatlemania, and the rise of fashionable hippydom, hairstyles had run riot. It's difficult to believe, when quite a lot of men in the first decade of the 21st century (in England at any rate) look as if they have escaped from Dartmoor, that in those days we all had pop-star-length hair. I have photographs of myself looking quite ridiculous, with sideburns down to my earlobes, a forehead so high that it reached the top of my head, and at the back a hairstyle which would have been more suited to a 1920s flapper.

I stopped laughing when I saw how crestfallen Richard was.

'You'll have to ask make-up to cut it for you,' I said.

'They just did,' he said.

You have to be really cruel sometimes.

One of the joys of our business is that nearly everybody is in love with their job. I took Terry Walsh out to the later location – a variation on the usual *Doctor Who* quarry.

If you've seen *Terror of the Autons*, you'll remember the occasion when one of the Auton policemen is knocked over the edge of a cliff by Mike Yates in the staff car, and does a splendid rolling tumbling fall down a 45-degree slope with a drop of at least 50 feet, and immediately starts to climb back up.

I needed this for the story, so that the gang could make their escape, but I was convinced that it was too dangerous for anybody actually to do it.

So I took Terry, who was going to play the Auton, out on a recce, and showed him a duplicate but short drop he could go flying over. I would then cut away to the getaway car, and then back to see him arriving at the bottom.

'No, no, ' says he, 'I'll do the whole thing.'

'Honestly, Terry, it could be really dangerous. And you'll get just as much money for the short fall.'

'I don't give a damn about the money,' he said. 'It's a marvellous stunt. I just want to have a go!'

This is the thing about stunt men. They never give you anything but 200 per cent. When I later did HG Wells's *The History of Mr Polly*, in a dream sequence Polly sees a knight in full armour on a rearing horse.

The stuntman did it a couple of times very successfully, and Lovett Bickford, the director, gave the go-ahead to move on.

'Oh, please let me have another shot at it! I'm sure I could make him rear up higher.'

And so he did. So high that the weight of the armour overbalanced the horse and it fell backwards, with its rider underneath. His foot was smashed.

He was still in hospital at the end of the shoot. I went to see him.

He was quite happy. He'd got his insurance and he was glad to have a rest – but most important he'd had a go.

When we came to the moment for Terry actually to do the fall I was as keyed up as if I were the one who was going to throw himself over the cliff.

Colin Davis, the conductor, once said to a less than sharp bunch of sopranoes, 'You should be waiting for the entry with so much energy inside that if anybody touched you, you'd explode!'

Just imagine what you must feel like just before a dangerous stunt.

And then the fool of a director, because he's all tensed up, shouts 'Action' before the cameras are turning and you **GO!!** and then have to **STOP!!!**

Heart pounding, your whole body flooded with adrenalin, you take up the opening position again, take a few deep breaths and…

'Turn over!'

'Sound running!'

'ACTION!'

It's a wonder Terry didn't break his neck because of my stupidity.

CHAPTER 18

No, it wasn't all plain sailing in the quarry.

Nobody has ever asked me why the Brigadier is wearing white socks with his uniform.

It wasn't as bad as when Dougie Camfield nearly collapsed, but from the same family. Nick arrived on the last morning of filming feeling pretty poorly but, trained in the hard school of 'the show must go on', he didn't tell anyone. But halfway through the day it was clear that he should be at home in bed.

So off he went, leaving his uniform behind for the suddenly promoted UNIT squaddie to change into. Which he smartly did, but in his haste forgot to change his socks. Which is why, when you see the back view of the Brig sprinting across the uneven ground during the fracas with the Autons, you get a tantalising flash of white.

I know the ground was uneven, because it was during the same shot that Katy twisted her ankle. That was when I learnt that those lovely big eyes saw the world like an Impressionist painting.

We managed. We put a line in about Jo Grant's limp, though I don't think it survived the edit.

And for the rest of the day, you saw only pieces of the Brigadier on the edge of shots; and his lines were parcelled out amongst the rest.

But you can understand why, at the end of the day, I was sitting in my car getting over it all when Michealjohn came over to entice me into joining him in his pyromania.

I watched the recording of *Terror of the Autons* the other day, and I was much cheered. As I told you, I felt that in many ways I screwed up quite a lot of the directing of *The Enemy of the World* – not all of it, by any means, but a significant part. So it was with a sense of relief that I pressed the eject button on the *Autons* video. After all these years, as a viewer it held me, though of course, there were things that I would now do differently.

For instance – and I can't think why the director didn't tell the producer that it should be changed – it's just plain daft that the Doctor is able to change the Master's mind about his plan merely by pointing out in one sentence that the Nestenes wouldn't treat him any differently from the rest of humanity.

Duh...

The Master! King of a defeated Earth!

The Master! Emperor of the Galaxy!

The Master! The Goofy to the Doctor's Mickey!

There was one shot which was a complete success; and so it should have been. It gave us more trouble than anything I've come across either before or since.

This is the shot of the scientist, played by Andrew Staines, who has been shrunk by the Master so that we see his tiny body lying in his own lunch box.

On the face of it it seemed simple enough. All we had to do was to put a piece of CSO blue material in the bottom of the box, and take a very high angle shot of Andrew lying on a floor that simulated the plastic of the box.

Put the two shots together and it would be bound to work.

Oh yes?

It looked as if we were seeing Andrew 20 feet away through a rectangular hole.

So we reversed the elements of the shot. Andrew sat on the blue CSO floor, leaning against the blue cloth, and we used the shot of the box as a background.

At least he now looked as if he were tiny, and actually in the box; but it was back to Loony Tunes. A brightly lit cartoon Andrew floated in free fall above the bottom of the box.

What was needed was a shadow. So they changed the lighting to give him one. But the equipment couldn't cope, and it frazzled and shimmered as if it was on fire. A good 30 minutes was spent trying to dowse it, but to no avail.

And then some genius thought of an answer.

If you've got a copy of the video, try holding the picture still and you'll see that he has a shadow, and that it does tie him down. It certainly works well enough for a shot that last so short a time.

He's sitting on an Andrew-shaped shadow cut out of brown paper.

All in all, the three-second shot took us two and a half hours – two hours in the afternoon to work it out, and then, because we didn't have a recording machine at the time, another half hour to line it up again in the evening because the electronic wind had veered to the north.

I used CSO for some shots, over three years after I'd left *Doctor Who*, when I produced and directed our own version of *Pinocchio* in 1978. It was adequate – just – for what I wanted, but poor old Pinoke still had to do without a shadow; and he looked more cartoony than the Disney version at times.

But in 1980 the backroom boys had cracked the problem, and I was able to fulfil a long-standing ambition of mine by doing *Gulliver in Lilliput*.

I'd loved the book since I found it in the library at the age of 12 and cycled home reading it on the handlebars.

In 1979, I saw a BBC show – the Arabian Nights, I think – and realised how much CSO had come on, and said to Graeme MacDonald in an unguarded moment, 'Now we could do Gulliver...'

'You're on!' he said.

It was just a passing thought; but there I was stuck with the most fiendishly difficult job imaginable. And to compound the foolishness, I said I'd dramatise it and direct it myself. Ron Craddock came across the corridor from his thriller serials to produce it ('You can permute any two jobs from three,' Graeme had said).

It turned out to be the best professional experience of my life; and this wasn't only because of the deep artistic satisfaction of being responsible for the entire thing, or the fun of working out how to make it look utterly real, but mostly because of the way everybody on the team made it their own.

Some time after this, when Terrance had joined me on the classic serial, we went to Albertine's wine bar for our lunch. Peter Moffat, who directed *The Five Doctors* (the sequel to our *Three Doctors)*, was sitting by the front door (in our usual corner, too) with a friend. We said hello.

'This is Terrance Dicks,' Peter said to his companion. 'He wrote my *Doctor Who*.'

'No, Peter,' said Terrance, 'You directed my *Doctor Who*!'

The thing is, they were both right. TV/film-making is a collaborative enterprise. But at its best it's not a question of each member of the team throwing their contribution into the pot and walking away, leaving the director to bring it to the boil by himself. No, the best results come when everybody owns the show 100 per cent.

This is how it was with *Gulliver in Lilliput*.

Without any prompting from me, for example, Dick Coles, who designed the sets, Amy Roberts, the costumes, and Pam Meager, the make-up, got together in a way I'd never experienced before. We'd fixed a style at our first planning meeting, setting it in 1726, the date of the book's publication; and agreed that it should be utterly real, but at the same time have an artificiality that mirrored the stylisation I had given the text, which was heavily influenced by the plays of the period.

I found, to my delight, that the wigs, the dresses and the sets were colour co-ordinated. Swatches of cloth, hanks of dyed hair and paint samples from the scene dock had been compared and matched exactly.

So what am I on about? What's this got to do with *Doctor Who*?

Lis Sladen (our Sarah Jane Smith) played Lady Flimnap, the Lord High Treasurer's wife, who causes a scandal, so Swift tells us, because she has been seen leaving Gulliver's dwelling late at night. Considering that she is only six inches tall, this might be thought to be carrying the shocked gossip of the court a little far.

Jenny McCracken, who was Claire in *Carnival of Monsters*, played her sister, Admiral Bolgolam's wife.

I had cast two superb actresses whose performances went a long way towards making *Gulliver* the success it was.

In working out our schedule, we separated the days with the simple scenes, shot in the usual way of drama, from those when we were doing the trick shots.

Although they were both playing leading roles, on the Saturday in question Lis and Jenny were needed only for one tiny scene, a bubbly conversation in the coach on their way to meet Gulliver for the first time. We were using CSO to put in the moving background behind the window, rather as back projection had traditionally been used. It's a dead simple process.

This simplicity was the trouble.

'When will you be needing them?' asked costume and make-up.

'Oh, certainly not before lunch,' I said. Lunch was at one o'clock.

In spite of the improvements in CSO, it was impossible to predict how long each setup would take to achieve. Each shot was planned to an inch, but sometimes things had to be changed radically to make them work, so, knowing that we could knock off the scene in the coach without any trouble, we kept postponing it until later in the day.

Unfortunately, 'just to be on the safe side', the two actresses had been wigged and made-up and, more to the point, squeezed into their tightly corseted dresses – authentic for 1726 – even before lunch. They found it impossible to eat, or sit down comfortably, and difficult to breathe easily.

They were eventually called onto the set to record the scene at five minutes to ten in the evening. Ten o'clock was the time we had to finish, and we'd been told we couldn't have an overrun under any circumstances.

Many actresses (and I could name a few, but I won't) would have been so angry that they would have refused to work under such pressure, but Lis and Jenny?

They put all their adrenalin into the excitement of the scene, summoned up all their reserves of professionalism and did it perfectly in one take.

Their generosity of spirit still brings tears to my eyes.

A couple of days after the last studio recording of *Terror of the Autons*, I had to take off the baseball cap of the director and don the producer's top hat again, as the location filming of *Mind of Evil* got under way.

Tim Combe was a good director, which was why I asked him back. But he did have one blind spot, which showed itself in both *The Silurians* and *Mind of Evil.*

The routine in those days, before the advent of video recording on location, was that the 16mm negative of each day's shoot was sent back to London by train. It was processed overnight and arrived with a 'rushes' print – what Hollywood calls the 'dailies' – at Ealing Studios, the centre of the BBC film operations, for the editor and the producer to view. Any comments, especially if they meant retakes, were passed on to the director by phone.

The last day of the *Silurians* shoot was at Marylebone railway station, where, in the story, people started collapsing from a mysterious plague.

I saw the rushes with Tim, as they'd wrapped the day before. The lights went up.

'Great stuff,' I said, and it was. 'Presumably there's another roll to come.'

'No, that's the lot. What do you mean?'

I was taken aback.

'Those high angle shots really work well,' I said, 'but didn't you take any close-ups, with the blotches on their faces and all that?'

No. He hadn't.

Yes, it told the story. But it was seriously undramatic, and this at a high point in the plot.

What could I do? We'd have to go back, but we were already way over the budget.

And then Lady Serendipity stepped in and arranged for a whole roll of film to be lost. It had been delivered to Ealing and was never seen again, presumably wrongly labelled and delivered to the wrong cutting room. Like a mis-filed document it would be impossible to trace it without opening every one of the hundreds of cans in the place.

Oh what a pity! We'd have to have another day's filming – and Ealing would have to pay for it!

We seized the opportunity to go back to the station and fill in the missing shots, braving the wrath of Equity by using people from the team instead of actors. Trevor, Terrance's then assistant, was one of them; and Sandra, our secretary, another.

So that was sorted.

See what I mean about having to keep an eye on everything?

And then, chase me Aunt Fanny rahnd the gasworks, if the poor blighter didn't go and do exactly the same thing in *Mind of Evil*! Twice.

Somebody who had been there in the fight for the missile told me that it was really exciting, and that Tim had cleverly covered the whole action in one developing shot.

My heart sank.

Sure enough, the next morning's rushes confirmed my fears.

Now, I've nothing against developing shots. Orson Welles, the master of them, showed us how effective they can be, with the incredible crane shot at the beginning of *Touch of Evil.* And what about Robert Altman's eight-minute tracking shot at the beginning of *The Player* which swoops from one tightish set up to another, and another, and another, never losing the framing or the drama of the story?

The trouble with Tim's was that it was all too loose. Again it lacked drama. And there was no way we could set up the day again, with the real rocket and troops.

And then came the battle at the prison, which was shot at Dover Castle.

Long shots. High angle shots. Wide shots. All beautifully planned, and executed – but there was hardly a close shot to be seen.

We couldn't afford it, but we went back to Dover for half a day. We saved money on our 'extras' in the same way as before. Legend has it that if you look carefully you can see Tim Combe shooting himself.

Serve him right.

He more than redeemed himself in my eyes when, with the editor, he cut together all the film he'd shot. *Mind of Evil* is a story with a complicated plotline, and maybe it suffers from the curse of the six-parter (not so heavy as the devil's work that is the seven-parter, but bad enough. Four episodes is best, five okay, but six nearly always sags) but it ended up with some of the most exciting scenes of our first two seasons

Whenever I directed, I scheduled myself at the beginning or the end of a season, so that my two jobs wouldn't clash too much. But this first time, I wasn't nearly as sorted out as I should have been.

A couple of things slipped by me, as producer. One was the horrendous cost of building a prison set with a real first floor gallery. I'd been taught a lesson with the Silurian caves about checking up, or so I thought. But I was obviously a poor pupil. It was already an enormously expensive show, with the gun-battle between the escaped convicts and UNIT troops, and the hijacking of a real ground-to-air missile. I had an overspend right at the beginning of the new season.

But that wasn't the only thing. I didn't keep a proper eye on Visual Effects. Luckily I visited their workshop in good time, and saw the Keller Machine, which housed the alien creature that the Master was using for his evil ends. Made of perspex, with flashing coloured lights inside, it was about as scary as a Christmas toy for a nine-year-old. It was redesigned, but the lack of time for the rebuild showed, I'm afraid.

But I didn't even see the monster which was supposed to frighten the Chinese Ambassador to death until it turned up in the studio. It had a great face, with savage fangs, but seen full-length it looked like an eight-foot pink quilted pyjama case.

Terrance immediately christened it 'Puff, the Magic Dragon' after the novelty song of the early 1960s.

Tim felt that we could get away with a long shot, but I insisted on it being seen only in close-up with plenty of smoke.

I'd learnt the hard way. Certainly, by the time we reached our third year, I managed to prevent Daisy, the cow-headed Minotaur, from reaching the screen. 'Oh, sorry,' said the freelance mask-maker. 'I thought cows and bulls looked the same.'

CHAPTER 19

Here's another little tip for neophyte producers: Never schedule a location film shoot on a bleak open beach in England ten days after Christmas.

You'd think it was obvious, wouldn't you?

Claws of Axos, that's what I'm talking about; the outcome of Terrance's protracted nursing of the Bristol Boys' story. The gigantic skull in Hyde Park in Bob and Dave's original had become a spaceship with an organic shape which had buried itself in the sand of the beach, which was very lucky for us, because we only had to build the entrance. But that's where our luck ran out.

Never mind the weather...

I'll rephrase that, because we were forced to mind the weather. No, it was something far more fundamental: the light. Mike Ferguson was the director and he found that he had to lose whole scenes, which were later shot as interiors, because there wasn't enough light to start much before 10am, and it was starting to get dark by 3.30pm. And as I say, the weather didn't help.

Terrance and I drove down to visit. As I told you, it's what producers do. But not many producers would be as silly as I was.

In those days I prided myself on not feeling the cold and, as I spent my time in centrally heated offices and studios and went everywhere by car, I didn't even own an overcoat. I stepped out into the wide open space that is Dungeness, into the bite of the wind that was blowing all the way from Siberia, and…

AAAARRRGH!!! as characters *in extremis* used to say in comics when I was a boy. (Do they still?)

Lord knows why the costume people had a long overcoat with a fur collar tucked away in the wardrobe van, but it undoubtedly saved my life, at the cost of making me look like a seedy actor-manager.

In the Navy we had an expression which encapsulated the farthest reach of selfishness: 'I'm all right, Jack, I'm inboard. Pull up the ladder!' and the first clause has become a cliché. So I was all right, Jack, but what about the PBA (poor bloody actors)?

Katy Manning, for example, was wearing a miniskirt with kneeboots; very Mary Quant. They were in a matching pale purple, deeper than a lilac, which suited her well, especially as her bare knees and thighs in between were exactly the same colour.

But it wasn't only the cold Mike had to contend with. During the five days the unit was filming, the overcast dullness would change to bright sunshine, to rain, to snow and to hail; and not just from day to day, but from hour to hour. Apparently the area is notorious for its versatile weather.

It soon became apparent to Mike that he would have to keep on shooting no matter what. There was no question of 'we'll have to wait for the sun' or '…until the sun goes in' or whatever. Just making sure that what he shot would cut together without too much of a jolt, he ploughed on regardless.

If we'd been shooting a normal drama we'd have been in trouble. 'Freak weather conditions have been reported in the area where the spaceship has landed,' the Brigadier was told back at UNIT HQ, when we shot the scene a couple of weeks later.

It's always possible that nobody would have noticed, except those with trained eyes. There've been, especially in TV films, such things as a bowling green where the wood left the bowler's hand in a dull overcast shot, only to arrive at the jack with a hard shadow from a bright sun.

To be honest, I was the director who had to accept that one, in a *Z Cars*.

But nobody seemed to be aware of it, so it makes the point.

What do you do when you have a disagreement with your boss?

Our boss Ronnie Marsh had some very strong opinions. Some were very idiosyncratic and could be ignored, or argued about, like his aversion to what the film world calls a dissolve (more properly a lap dissolve) when a picture fades out as another fades in on top of it. We in TV had got into the lazy habit of calling it a mix, as the sound people do.

'You can achieve nothing with a mix that can't be done better with a properly timed cut,' he used to say.

I think he was wrong. A mix is a very useful part of the grammar of telling stories on the screen. I used to argue with him, but I never convinced him.

He was a cheerful sort of man but he had a reputation for being ruthless and stubborn. And he did some insensitive things. But when I was a very new director, Judy, his wife, was my PA (known in those days as the director's secretary). She was one of the sweetest people I met at the Beeb. I cannot believe that she could have remained happily married to the man portrayed in the public perception of him.

I think he was a good-hearted man who was determined to make a success of the role he'd been cast in by Fate and the BBC bosses. Unfortunately he modelled his management style on his erstwhile boss in Light Entertainment, who had an even more Stalinist reputation.

I liked him; and he liked me. When I gave up *Who,* and he'd left Serials to become Head of the larger Series Department, he gave me a job as a sort of unofficial deputy looking at the many new projects that came in from the other producers, and from outside.

I soon gave it up. My position was invidious. I had responsibility but no power, and I found it most embarrassing to have my fellow producers treating me as a favourite at court. If I'd had ambitions that way, I could probably have parlayed myself into a real promotion, but the creative producer role was as far from the coalface as I wanted to go.

But it was good of Ronnie to give me the job, and he was very understanding when I said I wanted to go back to directing.

It was on *Claws of Axos* that I first crossed swords with him. Twice.

The first time I had to yield the day; the second, I ran him through with the sheer brilliance of my riposte. Well, that's the way it seemed to me.

The first was well within his remit as Head of Serials, representing the BBC editorially. We had a close-up of Pigbin Josh the tramp as his face just collapsed and melted away.

'It's far too horrific. I'm not having that going out at teatime on a Saturday!'

You're the boss, boss.

But the second…

We sec the inside of the spaceship at last, as Jo escapes: a stunning, surreal and psychedelic – and clearly organic and alive – interpretation of the Bristol Boys' concepts by Mike and the designer, Ken Sharp, working with the brilliant John Horton from Visual Effects.

'That goes on far too long,' says Ronnie. 'You must cut it down.'

I was taken aback. 'I don't think we have the right to change what Mike has done,' I said.

He frowned. 'The BBC doesn't give anybody the right to put anything they like on the air.'

'No, of course not. If it just didn't work, or it was too violent or something, it would be fair enough. But we've employed Mike to make artistic decisions. I think we should leave it the way he's edited it.'

Ronnie's only reply was a grunt. But I heard nothing more about cutting the sequence.

It was only afterwards that I remembered overruling Tim Combe's wide shot of Puff the Magic Dragon; and, now I come to think of it, on a later occasion insisting, much to Mike Briant's disgust, on losing large chunks of the electronic music in parts of *The Sea Devils* (because they sounded like sound effects, footsteps and gunshots, which could have been confusing). Both directors would no doubt have argued that I was making an aesthetic judgement.

I still think my criticisms were valid, but had I the moral right to use my clout as producer to insist?

I can't make up my mind.

Ronnie made two other editorial decisions of some consequence that second season. The second one, about the church at Devil's End, the village in *The Daemons*, was understandable; I should have thought of it myself. It could have landed us up to our collective necks in the village midden. I'll tell you about that later.

It was the first one, that concerned *Colony in Space*, that made me very angry – and brought up a point of principle that was fundamental to the way the BBC was structured.

I'll tell you why I stormed into his office – insofar as I ever stormed anywhere. I certainly knocked on the door, so perhaps it was more like half a gale (Force 7) than a real storm (Force 10). But not the way I was feeling inside.

This had come about because of the sort of story that *Colony in Space* was.

One of the things that Terrance and I quickly came to an agreement on was that stories which were nothing but a chase through the corridors with monsters weren't what we were looking for.

Not all that long after the launch of the first Pertwee season I got in touch with the BBC department Audience Research, and asked for a breakdown of the audience for *Who* in terms of age.

You'd never guess the answer. Well, perhaps you might, now it's become one of the most popular shows on British television. But it was a surprise in 1970.

Well over half – nearly 60% – were grown-ups; mothers with their kids, obviously, but the rest? *Doctor Who* was no longer just a children's programme.

So Terrance and I tried to take this on board in our planning. We tried to make each story work on several different levels at once:

- We'd have our BEMs (Bug-Eyed Monsters) to scare the children peeping over the back of the sofa (of course).
- We'd have an adventure action story with plenty of suspense.
- We'd have (if possible) an intriguing sci-fi extrapolation of current ideas, or a near-fantasy conflation of science and myth.
- We'd have a drama deriving from the interaction of characters you care about, who would talk to each other like real people, not like the cardboard drivers of the plot you'd get in shows like *Space 1999*.

- We'd have a story that had something to say, and wasn't just an interplanetary chaseabout or a disaster movie with giant slugs (or whatever).

The two last are most important to all good dramatic writing, though the latter will be by no means obvious in the finished article. But over and over again we'd read an outline or a synopsis submitted by a writer, and we'd say, 'Yes. Fine, a nice idea, and it could be exciting but... what is it *about*?'

That is to say, what is its theme? What point does it make?

This is not to say that it had to have a message, though it might. *The Green Death*, for example, was explicitly planned to call attention (in *Who*-ish terms) to the pollution that uncaring big business can bring about.

But *Robot*, the first Tom Baker story, which Terrance wrote, wasn't only an affectionate *hommage* to *King Kong*, but also took a look at the development of artificial intelligence and asked questions (by implication) about the nature of consciousness and personal identity, with a side swipe at the sort of political arrogance that gives birth to the far right in all its nastiness.

But no matter what the theme, it would never be up front, lecturing the audience (as the man said, 'If you want to send a message, use Western Union'); but it would be there as a unifying subtext to inform the structure.

Colony in Space is full of *Who*-ish elements: monster lizards; a race of Primitives with a strange Guardian ruling them; a doomsday weapon; and of course, this being his first season, the Master, eager to get hold of it and hold the whole galaxy to ransom. But the underlying theme is undoubtedly political. It has a great similarity to those Westerns that show unscrupulous ranchers throwing small farmers off their land; or the tales we read in the papers about development companies buying up homes where people have lived all their lives and winkling them out.

In our case, it's the Interplanetary Mining Corporation versus the colonists.

And though there's the odd goodie-baddie, the real villain of the piece, Morgan, is a vicious nasty who thoroughly enjoys his persecution of the settlers.

When Michael Briant, as director, settled down with the scripts of *Colony in Space* to think about the casting, he had a bright idea. He was full of them.

'Why not make Morgan a woman?' he said.

Mmm…

It would certainly make a change from the usual female villain, slinky, sensual and seductive (in the nicest possible way). The IMC people were to wear uniforms and jackboots, to emphasise their difference from the colonists who were more like simple peasants.

'Why not? Good thinking, Batman!'

So Michael went ahead and cast Susan Jameson with my full approval.

I'd always liked her work.

It wasn't until the casting was almost finished that Ronnie got round to reading the scripts.

And blew up.

'A sadistic female with a whip striding about the place in kinky boots murdering people! In *Doctor Who*? Change it back!'

Maybe I've invented the whip, but he certainly said, 'kinky boots'.

So Tony Caunter, who'd been cast as one of the more junior members of the IMC, would suddenly find himself promoted, and Susan would be paid for not doing a job – frustrating, but at least it would pay a few bills.

Ronnie's edict came well within the brief of the Head of Department's editorial function, representing the BBC. End of story.

End of story? Not quite.

Let me explain.

For many years, from the first beginnings of the BBC, when the British Broadcasting Company Ltd (started in 1922 by the manufacturers of radios to give their customers something to listen to, with John Reith as Managing Director) became in 1927 the British Broadcasting Corporation with a Royal Charter, it was run by its producers and editors. Under Reith's watchful eye, they were the ones who decided what they were going to put on the air.

When the organisation expanded to the point where they put forward their ideas to a Head of Department (usually one of their brother producers), they still kept a great deal of autonomy – and this remained the case even when radio's little brother, television, outgrew its sibling and became the giant it was in my time on *Doctor Who*.

As I've told you, Graeme MacDonald was for a while the Head of Serials. He was well-liked, and when he died at an early age his memorial service was packed.

I was in the second row of pews, and in the middle of the front row sat John Birt, at the time Director General of the BBC.

The prestigious director Christopher Morahan had been asked to deliver a eulogy. As is the custom, he ran through Graeme's career, which was remarkable, with him ending up as Controller of BBC2; the first person from the drama department ever to rise so far up the hierarchy.

But Christopher concentrated on Graeme's time as producer of the *Wednesday Play/Play for Today* strand, when he was responsible, not only for a number of

Dennis Potter's early plays, but also for such gems as Jack Rosenthal's *Bar Mitzvah Boy* and *Spend Spend Spend*. His reign was notable for its independence, often challenging the accepted norm, and even hitting the headlines.

'But of course,' said Christopher, looking straight through John Birt, 'that was in the days when the BBC trusted its producers.'

Few realise just how big the Corporation was (is?). If the MD Tel of my day had watched every programme produced by the BBC – not even counting the ones bought in – he'd have had no time to do anything else, and precious little home life.

There was a survey done by a team of Management Consultants about this time, and in their report they said that they had never come across an organisation that had so many decision makers.

The BBC wasn't an autocracy, ruled from the top, it was a loose collection of largely independent fiefdoms. We were given the resources, and left alone to get on with it. And we were very jealous of our prerogatives as the sovereigns of our little kingdoms.

This was why I was so angry with Ronnie, and 'stormed' into his office.

On RE day (Ronnie Explosion), I was late coming in. Maybe I'd had to go to a viewing of *Claws of Axos*, which was in production at the time; or maybe I'd had some family chores to do.

I was paid to exercise judgement and make decisions, not to sit in an office. That was my secretary's job, or part of it. If I wanted to be late, nobody had the right to criticise, not even Ronnie.

When I arrived – about 11.30 it would be – I checked in with Sandra and then wandered along to the *Colony in Space* production office to see how things were going, to find Mike and his PA scrambling to sweep up the mess left by Ronnie's bombshell.

I walked straight out, down the stairs to the next floor, into the outer office, with its two secretaries, one with a big desk and one with a small one – yes, that's how grand Ronnie's role was; even his secretary had a secretary…

'Is he alone?'

She looked startled. 'Yes, but…'

I did knock on the door, but I didn't wait for his 'Come in!'

'I gather you've told Mike Briant to recast our villain.'

He looked up from the script he was reading.

'I did. I'm not having…'

'You had no right to do that.'

Now he was angry. 'What do you mean? I have every right to change things!'

'Yes, of course. But you've no right to go over my head to the director. You should have come and told me. *I'm* the producer of *Who*.'

There was a principle at stake: not only concerning the producer's precious historical autonomy, but also his authority as the one carrying the ultimate responsibility for the programme, which shouldn't be undermined.

But was it also my affronted Ego that was speaking? (I didn't shout.)

Yes, of course it was. The steam coming out of Ego's ears was no doubt misting up the clarity of my thinking.

Certainly I can remember very little of the rest of our exchange. He didn't give way, and I didn't give way. And the next time we met we treated each other with a wary friendliness, and soon relaxed.

I don't feel angry about it now. If I had been in his position I might have felt as he did.

But I still think I was right.

CHAPTER 20

So what was the last royal command that year from our Liege Lord on the floor below? All in good time. Suffice it to say that it concerned *The Daemons.*

This was the last story of the second season, and as I told you, it was a spinoff... no, that's the wrong word... a development of the black magic scene I'd written for the Jo Grant auditions.

And when Terrance suggested that I should write the story myself I jumped at the idea.

But there was a snag. You had to ask permission to write for your own programme.

Recently the Writers' Guild had started flexing its muscles, complaining about this practice, and what was known as 'commissioning down the corridor', where staff members employed each other; so the BBC was being very sticky about the whole thing.

I daren't risk a finger-wagging Auntie saying no to me. Quite apart from my Orson Welles complex, I desperately needed the money.

The obvious answer was to find a front man, a struggling writer who would be willing to put his name to my script for a small percentage of the fee.

But quite apart from the stink it would raise if I was found out, I could never have brought myself to be as devious as that. It went against all my instincts.

Freud would no doubt have said that I'd successfully internalised my superego.

In any case, how could I pretend to be trying to follow the teachings of the Buddha, if I were to contravene so comprehensively at least three of the sections of the Eightfold Path: Right Action; Right Speech; and Right Livelihood.

But I saw no moral reason why I shouldn't have a go if I could find a more legitimate way. After all, if I'd asked the bosses, I might have caught them in a good mood, so I would be dealing with a technicality.

But how? Ah, of course! Collaboration.

But it would be somewhat insulting to tell whoever it was the reason…

This was when I decided that I would be (what I call) openly Machiavellian.

I would leave it until the collaboration was well under way, and obviously a success, and then tell him.

I say just 'him' rather than adding 'or her' because I'd already made up my mind who I was going to ask. Who else but my old *Skyport* mate, Owen Holder?

He'd moved into the country, so I hadn't seen him for some time. I gave him a ring.

'How'd you like to get together to write a *Doctor Who*?'

'Mmm… science fiction's not really my thing. In any case, I'm rather busy at the moment.'

I asked him if he could possibly fit it in.

'Barry, I'm sure you're quite capable of writing it by yourself.'

He was perfectly friendly about it, but quite immovable – and I could hardly tell him the whole story.

Right then, who else? There was really nobody I knew well enough. I talked to Chummy about it.

'Why don't you ask Bob Sloman?' she said.

At this time she was working at a local playgroup. Mary Sloman was there too, and we'd become friends with her and Bob. He and I shared a lot of interests, including sailing.

Bob had been an actor himself, meeting Mary in rep. But he'd given it up and got himself a steady job – indeed a career – with the circulation department of the *Sunday Times*.

But his real vocation was writing, and he never stopped. Apart from the usual radio plays and so on, he'd had two plays on in the West End, *The Golden Rivet* and *The Tinker*, which was turned into a film, *The Wild and the Willing*.

It was an inspired suggestion, and Bob dived in with all the enthusiasm he always gave to his favourite activities, sailing and flying. And when I revealed my Machiavellian secret some time later, he laughed.

Writing *The Daemons* was an extraordinary time. We were determined to get all the details of the witchcraft right, so we steeped ourselves in every book we could find, and then met to discuss what we'd uncovered. After a few sessions, we started seeing Devils wherever we turned.

No, not an imp with vestigial horns and a barbed tail, wearing a scarlet leotard and clutching an outsize toasting fork; I'm talking about everyday sights which revealed hitherto hidden patterns which could be mistaken for nothing else.

For example, Chummy and I had a decorative plate on the wall – from Spain, I think it was – with an abstract design on its face.

Abstract? Not a bit of it. If it wasn't Satan himself staring at me as I ate my breakfast, it was certainly one of his henchmen.

And clouds which with earlier eyes might have seemed almost in the shape of a camel, glared at us malevolently from an otherwise pastoral sky.

I would guess that one of the reasons for the recognised image of the Devil was the habit of the early church of transmogrifying pagan practices and iconography into Christian symbols, such as the purloining of the Saturnalia celebrations and attaching them to Jesus's birthday. How else to explain the pronounced family resemblance of the Devil to the Great God Pan, with his horns and his cloven hooves?

Though of course, as the Doctor explains in our story, horns have been a symbol of power for many eons. Michelangelo even sculpted a statue of Moses with horns.

Damaris Hayman who played our white (i.e. good) witch said to me, 'I suppose you had to call him the Horned Beast; after all, you couldn't say the Horned God without offending half your audience.'

In fact, it had never even occurred to us to refer to the Devil, in his goatish form, as the Horned God.

She also complimented us on the accuracy of our references to witchcraft rituals and forms, such as 'consulting the talisman of Mercury', and 'casting the runes'. Like a lot of good actresses, she'd been doing a spot of research.

It has been said that in writing *The Daemons* we borrowed heavily from Nigel Kneale's *Quatermass and the Pit*. Though there are similarities, the truth is somewhat different.

Terrance and I were agreed that we didn't want a straight black magic story. As in our later foray into 'going back to the past' with *Time Warrior*, we felt it had to have a strong science fiction element.

Both Bob and I had thoroughly enjoyed (and been half convinced by) Erich von Daniken's bestseller *Chariots of the Gods*, which presented the thesis, backed up by archaeologically unexplained oddities from all over the world, that alien beings had landed on Earth in prehistoric times and had set *Homo sapiens* on his way.

When we discovered that there was a parallel belief, in certain witchcraft traditions, that angels had come down to procreate with the humans of the time, producing the precursors of modern man, we knew that we'd found our green umbrella.

But there was an obvious similarity to the Quatermass story. In those days, we didn't have video cassettes (let alone 10,000 songs dancing on the head of a pin-sized iPod), so we couldn't go down the road and get the film version to look at…

Oh yes, we could. It was showing in the suburbs somewhere. So off we went to the pictures.

It's all go, our job.

The object wasn't to pinch Nigel Kneale's ideas. Quite the opposite. We wanted to make sure that our version was different. Obviously there would have to be something of the same jumping-off point – the discovery of a buried spaceship; but after that the two stories take off in entirely different directions.

At the time, nobody but Terrance knew that I was the co-author. Bob and I hatched a *nom de plume* to go on the title sequence: Guy Leopold. Guy is the name of his son, and Leopold, my middle name, was the surname of my mother's grandfather who, early in the 19th century, fled with his brother (to escape conscription) from Fürth, a little town near Nuremburg, to the Channel Islands.

What's that got to do with the price of…

No. I can't use that one again. It's severely out of date anyway.

But what has my great grandfather got to do with a *Doctor Who* story? I'll tell you, because it has quite a lot to do with my fascination for time, and time-travel sci-fi.

Don't you find it extraordinary that in only two or three generations I can jump back nearly 200 years?

When Great Grandpa Louie came to Jersey, the battle of Waterloo was nearer to him than the turn of the millennium is to us.

We are living in history.

For that matter, I was born less than seven years after the end of the First World War. I can remember, as a small boy, the lamplighter with his long pole, coming up the road in the evening to turn on the gas in the street lamps; I can remember feeding lumps of sugar to Jones, the horse who pulled the baker's delivery van; I can remember Mr Glover, the milkman, pushing his little cart with its giant wheels at the back, dipping his ladle into the great milk churn suspended between them to fill the can which he brought to our back door, to ladle a pint or two into our jug…

If this isn't history, what is?

One of the parts I played as a theatre actor was Stephen Langton, the Archbishop who was involved with King John's quarrel with Rome and his signing of the Magna Carta, in a play written by the poet Patrick Dickinson. As with the first performances of TS Eliot's *Murder in the Cathedral*, it was to be performed in the Chapter House of Canterbury Cathedral.

We were to use a room in the Archdeacon's house as our dressing room, and had a free run of the grounds.

A couple of days before the first night, the after-lunch rehearsal having been cancelled, I went into the garden to enjoy my unexpected freedom. Protected by the precinct walls from the sound of the traffic, the quietness was broken only by the occasional murmur of a bee. My mind was still in the early 13th century.

I was sitting on an ancient seat made out of large stones, probably left over from the building of the Cathedral; and as I breathed in the utter peace I realised that there was nothing I could see that wouldn't have been there when Archbishop Langton was alive.

He could have sat on that very same stone.

He might walk round the corner at any moment.

Time vanished. Stephen Langton was as close to me as Charles, my father-in-law, who had died some four years earlier, or Grandpa Louie, who'd lasted into the 1890s.

This morning is very like yesterday morning. I had the same coffee in the same cup; sure, the news in the *Guardian* was different, but the paper looked the same; if I walk up to the High Street this afternoon the other shoppers won't be wearing period clothes, or the odd garb we science fictioneers are apt to inflict on our actors if they stray even 20 or 30 years into the future.

Nothing is particularly different, it would seem, from day to day.

And yet there have been enough changes to ensure that the inexorable march of history continues. Everything is changing, all the time. Unnoticeably.

There is an unbroken link between us and the past. Our personal histories and those of our forebears, and the genes that we share, reach back through the centuries, day by day, until they touch the very first creatures who might be called human.

The present moment may be all that exists, but it holds within itself the whole of existence since the Big Bang.

So Guy Leopold wrote *The Daemons.* Then we decided that this was a bit silly, as Bob was signing the contracts and receiving the money. So the rest of the ones we wrote together were credited to Robert Sloman.

There would have been no reason why we shouldn't have kept up the public deception indefinitely. But three of the four stories were great successes.

(I would agree that *The Time Monster* is flawed in a number of ways.) *The Daemons* itself was consistently voted by the fans the best of all *Who* productions, only being dethroned by Terry Nation's masterpiece, *Genesis of the Daleks*, in the Tom Baker era.

I said at the beginning that I'd do my best to be honest with you. I was jealous that Bob was getting all the applause. So, much later, when it really didn't matter either way, I came out as his secret other half.

Mark you, that doesn't imply that most of the credit was really due to me. It was a true collaboration. As with Terrance, neither Bob nor I would be able to tell you who came up with what idea; and the actual dialogue was sometimes Bob's and sometimes mine.

We would start off with brainstorming sessions, just throwing in relevant – and sometimes not so relevant – suggestions. Occasionally Bob's sense of humour would get the better of him and he'd come up with something that had a scabrous note that, if it had made it to the final recording, would infallibly have finished my career.

For example, when we decided, being responsible fellows (or at least wary), that it wouldn't be a good idea when the Master is calling up the Devil (really Azal, the goat-horned alien) for him to recite the Lord's Prayer backwards as in the Black Mass, he suggested that instead we should reverse *Eskimo Nell.* For those who don't know it, I'll just explain that it is not the sort of verse you'd bring out as your party piece at the Vicar's tea table.

We settled for the old nursery rhyme, *Mary Had a Little Lamb*, instead.

Once we'd got a main story outline, we'd start at the beginning again and work out a scene-by-scene breakdown for each episode. When we and Terrance were happy with it, Bob would take it away and use it as a basis to write the whole thing.

You see, unlike me, Bob wrote very fast, just letting it gush out in a torrent of words. This sometimes led to inspired chunks, and sometimes to bits that were frankly clunky.

He never checked it, or edited it. He'd just hand it over to me, episode by episode, and say, 'There you are. Do what you like with it.'

So I did. I worked my way through it, rewriting scenes where I felt the dialogue could be improved, or restructuring anything that seemed to have collapsed under the weight of his words. But I would leave his best bits severely alone.

Every episode turned out too long, and I handed them over to Terrance to edit. He has a dictum, 'Anything can be cut, and cutting will always improve it.'

I don't agree. What can happen is that the quirky bits, the bits with a bit of fun in them, are stripped away, leaving the bare bones of the plot. But it's certainly true that the original writer always finds it well nigh impossible to lose any of his precious words – and sometimes the ones he loves most are the very ones that need to go.

As the man said, the best way to edit is to 'kill your darlings'.

On the other hand…

I wandered into Terrance's office to see how he was getting on with the edit. I looked over his shoulder. His 'blue pencil' was poised over a bit of Bob's dialogue.

'Oh, please don't cut that!' I said.

'Okay,' he said.

It became the Brigadier's most famous line:

'Chap with wings there, five rounds rapid…'

CHAPTER 21

Memory's a funny thing. It's not just the library we consult for facts, or the cinema where we star in a never-ending soap.

Together with our genes, it's what makes us who we are.

We've all read of those unfortunates who forget everything... Ah but they don't, do they? If they were to lose the lot, they'd be lying on the floor, kicking, as helpless as a new-born baby.

Their amnesia – known as a fugue – is highly selective. They don't forget how to walk, or talk, or use a knife and fork. They just forget their own personal history. And lose themselves.

One of the mechanisms for building the sense of self is the way the brain operates as an editor of the perceptions coming in through the medium of the senses – and the memories of those perceptions. Everything that hits the brain has to be interpreted by comparison with our previous experience; and it's been shown over and over again that the interpretations can be very wide of the mark. Look at the way witnesses of an incident can contradict each other.

We add, we subtract, we subtly angle 'facts' to make ourselves look good – and this with no intention of deceit. And every time we have a memory, we reinforce the (possible) mistakes until the story it tells is set in stone.

I know I've got a good memory for the long-gone past. My first memory is of sitting in a high chair, with a mess of mashed-up egg and bread in my dish, feeling proper grumpy because my brother, two years older, is sitting at the table eating a real boiled egg with dippers (we didn't call them soldiers). I couldn't have been more than three years old, possibly less.

And the rest of my life is vivid to me at every stage. It seems to me that every detail is absolutely accurate.

Yet, twice in my recollections of *Who* I find that I have a different memory of the course of events from those of the other players in the particular bit of the tale.

It would be considerably more than two, but I leave out Jon, because his editing was so flagrant that it was difficult to believe that it wasn't deliberate.

For example, when we were shooting the famous chase in *Planet of the Spiders* he insisted, as I knew he would, on driving the one-man hovercraft himself – after all, it was Jon who had suggested that we have it in the show; and I believe he bought it afterwards and took it out to his place in Ibiza.

Now, the big thing that you have to take into account when steering a hovercraft is that, unlike a boat, it doesn't have a keel and a rudder; or rather, its rudder isn't in the water but in the air, in the slipstream of the driving propeller, like the rudder of a propeller-driven aircraft.

If you try to alter course in a plane without banking, its inertia will tend to carry you along in your original direction. It's like trying to steer a car round a corner at speed on a very icy road.

You skid.

The same thing happens with a hovercraft. So you have to take a very wide sweep when you want to change direction. It makes it very difficult to control.

So when we got down to the location, Jon seized every opportunity to practise.

Very sensible.

And when he came in to have his lunch, having thoroughly enjoyed himself scooting up and down the River Severn, he said to me, 'Why don't you have a go, Barry? But be careful. It's tricky to steer.'

So off I went; and it was. But, just as Jon had, I soon got the hang of it. I had great fun, and brought it back in time to get my own lunch and talk through the afternoon's work with the production manager.

This included Jon cutting off a corner to catch up with the villain in his motorboat by driving the hovercraft off the water, over the top of the bank, across a field and down the other side onto the water again.

Just to add to the joy of nations, I stationed a sleeping tramp the other side of the first bank, so that the Doctor would drive right over him.

When we came to shoot it, there was no point in rehearsing, so we had to have two takes, because Jon found the first time that he should have started his turn much earlier, to allow for the sideslip; he missed the tramp by about ten yards.

So we went again, as we say. And this time, Jon, being very expert in controlling any mechanical vehicle (he'd raced cars and hydroplanes for a few years when he was younger) found the exact line, and drove over Stuart Fell as planned.

Now, this is the version that Jon used to tell at conventions:

'...so when I came in to have my lunch, I said to Barry, "It's very tricky to steer, you know," and he said, "Oh, it can't be as difficult as all that," so I said, "Well, why don't you have a go yourself?" – and we spent the rest of the lunch hour watching Barry desperately trying to bring the thing back to the shore...'

And then he'd go on to describe the set-up with the sleeping tramp.

'The first time, I came up so far from Stuart that I knocked the camera over; and the cameraman as well.

'So we had to have another go. and this time I came over at the right place. But what I didn't know was that Barry, to be on the safe side, had moved the camera. I hit it again, and broke it!'

Well, I suppose it makes a good story.

So who are the two that I differ from in our accounts, who I agree have the right to argue that their version is the correct one?

Terrance, who remembers the details of our setting up our first Dalek story, *Day of the Daleks,* quite differently from me; and Chris Barry, over the filming of *The Daemons.*

Ever since the cancellation of *Snowy Black* I'd hankered after my plan to have a go at multiple shooting on location. And when I came to write *The Daemons* with Bob, I had a bright idea.

Well, I thought it was at the time. Was it?

Yes it was. It was worth doing, but by no means cheap; and very complicated to set up. You wouldn't want to do it all the time.

There was no way we could use the Outside Broadcast cameras, with their retinue of furniture vans, on a *Who* shoot. To move them around was a major operation. After all, once they were installed at a football or a tennis match – or in Westminster Abbey – they could stay put. It was only possible to use them for drama if you weren't going to have more than one or two locations. By its very nature, *Who* always demanded more.

But why shouldn't we take three 16mm film cameras, locked together electronically so that their shutters opened in synch? Then, instead of using a vision mixer to cut on the run, as we did with video cameras, we could edit the sequences later in the normal filmic way.

It would be expensive; but the above-the-line cost, the real cash cost, would be largely due to the enormous shooting ratio: the amount of film stock used in relation to the amount of screen time shot. If I allowed for that in the budget, we could shoot a lot of scenes (that would have normally been put into the studio) in a fraction of the time the single camera method would take.

And that would mean that we could open up the story and have much more of it outside.

So, in writing it, Bob and I deliberately planned the structure to take this into consideration. Not only was there far more filming than in a normal *Who* but the scenes were tailored to fit.

The intention was that the cameramen would wear earphones, and the director would be lurking out of shot, with a microphone in his hand, giving them directions as the scene was played.

'Three, as soon as he sits, zoom in to the close-up. When he rises, let him go... Stand by, Two, he's going to rise into your shot. Pan left with him as he goes to the gate...'

This was normal practice in the multi-camera video studio, with the director sitting in the gallery. The moves would have been rehearsed, of course, but these reminders meant that the cameramen didn't have to keep looking at their shot lists, or crib cards.

When I asked Chris Barry to direct, I explained all this to him. I could hardly lumber him with all the extra work this way would entail without warning him. He was very enthusiastic about it. So that was all right.

That's my version.

Chris, on the other hand, has said that he'd always wanted to try the multiple film-camera way of shooting, and when he got our scripts and saw how much location work there was, he decided to ask if he could have a go.

We can't ask Bob to give us his memory of how it was as sadly he died in 2006. But apart from my memory of our script meetings, the budget for the season would have had to have been planned long before Chris joined.

Never mind. It doesn't really matter. Chris did a great job under great pressure (including snow at the end of April), and used the new method of filming to enormous advantage.

This brings us neatly to the last big 'No!' pronounced by Ronnie in that second season.

The climax of the story, as I intimated earlier, was the raising of the 'Devil' by the Master; and we included the threat of a human sacrifice – Jo Grant, of course, tastefully covered in a linen tabard, rather than stretched out naked on the altar, as in the more lurid illustrations of Devil worship. I thought of this when Katy later turned up in her birthday suit peeping round a Dalek for the centre spread of a top-shelf magazine. Perhaps she'd been disappointed by our discretion?

Legend has it that black magicians, Satanists, would hold their version of the Mass in the local church (at midnight, when all good vicars are asleep).

Though our ritual wasn't a black Mass, Bob and I situated it in the church at Devil's End, the village at the centre of our story; and Chris's team had found the perfect location at Aldbourne in Wiltshire, which had an ancient village green with a pub on one side, which became our Cloven Hoof, and a little church sitting on its hillock at the far end.

Off they went, and I'm pretty sure that they started with all the stuff that concerned the church itself: the opening sequence of the tower at night, lit up by lightning flashes; the Brigadier with his UNIT squad besieging the churchyard after Azal has been raised inside; Bok, the living stone gargoyle, keeping guard and vapourising any soldier who came too near; the Doctor braving its evil powers to make his way to the sacristy door; and everybody inside, Master, Doctor, Jo and Mike, and the whole coven of ensnared villagers, rushing to escape when the end of Azal is about to blow the roof off the church…

Whether this was the first location or not, you can see that it featured very largely in the story. To have decided, after Chris had started his shoot, that we would locate the Master's ritual somewhere else, would have been impossible.

Yet this is what Ronnie Marsh demanded. The scripts had been on his desk for weeks, but he only got round to reading them the day after the team had started filming. In spite of all the care we had taken to make sure that nothing actually blasphemous happened, he was adamant.

'You will not shoot those scenes in a church; and that's that!' he said.

I couldn't even argue. He was acting within his brief as Editor/Executive Producer/Head of Department, representing BBC policy.

Controlled panic stations…

Terrance and I dropped everything else and went into closed session, but soon found that we were discarding every option that we could think of as utterly impractical. If the church had been used in one or two scenes only, we could have done a quick rewrite, added a couple of days to the schedule and gone to have a large drink. But it wasn't just a large part of the filming, it was a major ingredient of the whole story.

Our talk was punctuated by long silences.

'What if…?'

No.

'Suppose they…'

No, no.

'The Master could...'

No, no, no...

I have no idea where the brilliant suggestion came from that not only solved our problem at a stroke but was a better idea than the one that Bob and I had had in the first place. I like to think that I thought of it, of course, but then, I would, wouldn't I? It's just as likely to have been Terrance's inspiration.

We didn't have to change the filming an iota. It wouldn't even cost any more.

So what was the solution; and how did it improve on the original?

Remember, when I was talking about the appearance of the Devil, with his horns and his cloven hooves, that I brought up the way the early Church built on local pagan traditions? Well, what better symbol of this than that the Devil's End church was originally built on top of a large cavern that had been used for pagan worship from the earliest times?

And if the only way into it was through a door in the sacristy, which you would think would lead into a crypt, then nothing we were shooting on film would have to be changed.

The Daemons had a new depth to it. In every sense.

CHAPTER 22

So here we are at the end of our second season, which is where I always intended to end this first volume.

Starting at the beginning, let me walk through my memories and see if there's anything left by the wayside that I meant to pick up.

Here's one for a start:

Jon called any words even vaguely scientific or technical 'scientific gobbledygook', especially if it was of any length. At the beginning of rehearsals on any story, we would have a round-the-table readthrough of all the scripts, which Terrance and I would go to, together with key members of the production team such as the costume designer and make-up.

Afterwards, Jon would come up to Terrance, saying, 'I can't possibly say that. I'd never remember it, apart from anything else.'

Terrance would smooth down his ruffled feathers and simplify it a bit; but even then he wouldn't be happy until he'd worked out a way of coming to terms with it.

The most famous of these lines was very early on.

John just couldn't get his tongue round it – until he discovered its rhythm; and he started to dance round the rehearsal room singing it to the tune of the last phrase of the sailor's hornpipe.

'Reverse the polarity of the neutron flow.'

It's more than gobbledygook, it's scientific rubbish. The whole point of a neutron is that it has no polarity. If the line had come up later in my time as producer, I would have cut it on sight.

As it was, it became a sort of lucky talisman; and we introduced it into show after show, just for the fun of it.

It's very difficult to get an accurate timing of a script in the office. So much depends on how the actors will speak their lines. So, at this readthrough, a first rough timing would be done; and, if there were large differences from the right length, cuts (pre-decided, just in case) would be made, or Terrance would make a note for more dialogue to be written.

The latter didn't happen all that much, but over time, Terrance developed a foolproof method of inserting some extra drama.

You remember the dictum, 'Drama is conflict?' Aristotle, wasn't it? If it wasn't it ought to have been.

Terrance just wrote ding-dong quarrel scenes. Foolproof, and the actors loved them.

If we knew beforehand that we had substantial cuts, we tried to make certain they'd been made by the time the actors got the scripts. Otherwise, sure as eggs aren't little apples, one of them, probably dear old Nick Courtney, would pipe up, 'You're cutting my best bit.'

Indeed, on one occasion – in *Beau Geste* it was, not *Who* – we were overrunning, so Terrance cut in half a scene which was little more than some inconsequential chat between a bunch of legionnaires. But then one of them rather diffidently approached Terrance, and said, 'Please, please, don't cut those two lines. Please!'

Terrance looked where he was pointing in the script. The lines didn't seem particularly memorable.

'Why not?'

'Because it's my whole part!'

What was all that about Zen?

Its real impact on the Doctor comes later on. I'll tell you more about that next time, when we get to *Planet of the Spiders*.

But the impact on me was another matter. During this period I was busy arguing myself out of the Catholic Church, to which I'd doubtfully converted in 1954.

Unlike one of the most famous converts of the 20th century, the contemplative monk Thomas Merton, who managed to reconcile his orthodoxy with his recognition of the clarity of the Zen way of looking at the world, I found the intellectual contradictions of the basic dogmas made them simply incredible.

For example, I could accept the idea of Hell as a philosophical necessity as the antithesis of Heaven: a freely chosen total separation from God. But I couldn't believe that a loving Father would allow any of his children to place themselves in eternal torment.

Free will? If God is all-knowing, at the moment of the act of creation he is aware of everything that will follow, through to the end of time, including the 'freely chosen' rejection of him by those who will end up in Hell. To my mind, that lays the responsibility for their eternal torture squarely on him.

For that matter, think about the concept of free will for a bit; and if you come up with an answer to the problems it poses that satisfies the philosophers, they'll institute a Nobel prize in Philosophy, just for you.

But in any case, how could I come to terms with a God who, however angry he is with the beings he has created, can only be propitiated by a blood sacrifice, a human sacrifice, the slaughter of his only begotten son? It would take a Saddam Hussein, or an Idi Amin, to insist on such a harsh satisfaction in real life.

I found that the books of theology I read in an attempt to understand were full of attempts to gloss over or explain away these very real concerns.

I was dropping items of the creed, one by one, until I came to the point where I was merely saying, 'I believe in God' and keeping silent as the rest of the congregation completed it. And when I found that a question mark had crept in, I realised it was time to follow where my mind and my heart were leading me.

And that was towards the pureness, the simplicity (once it's understood) and the mystery of the teaching of Gautama Siddartha in its Zen incarnation and Zen's cousin, Vipassana, or Insight Meditation.

One of the beliefs of the Buddhist world is that the core teaching, the possibility of awakening to reality, and how that awakening can come about, is discovered over and over again throughout history.

In our galaxy – the Milky Way – alone there are billions of stars. If every star was a grain of salt, they would fill an Olympic swimming pool. And there are billions of galaxies in the universe. I find it difficult to believe that our little planet is the only one containing intelligent life. The sort of 'religion' that I can find acceptable is one that could be discovered anywhere in the universe, being based on evidence and experience, rather than the interpretation of a myth.

And 'anywhere in the universe' would of course include Gallifrey, if it existed.

A Zen master might be asked how different his life is from those who aren't awakened.

'When I draw water, I draw water. When I chop wood, I chop wood,' he might answer.

But doesn't everybody do that?

Not a lot. When we're doing the washing up, we're thinking about the cup of tea we're going to have afterwards, perhaps; and as we drink our tea, we're going through yet again the argument we had with our boss, and worrying about it, or looking forward to the holidays or...

So all we've got to do is live for the moment. Way-hay! Wine, women and song. Great!

Wrong.

Living *for* the moment isn't quite the same as living *in* the moment.

There is a phrase in Zen: 'a taste of *kensho*'. *Kensho* could be translated as 'knowing' or 'seeing', as when one suddenly sees the answer to a puzzle.

I can't give you that immediate sense of it, but maybe I can point a finger at where to look for it.

In the book version of *The Daemons*, I was able to expand a bit on the script. The Doctor is driving Bessie, his little yellow car, with Jo as his passenger, from the village out to the heat barrier that the Daemon has created and...

Why don't I just let you read it for yourself?

...poor Bessie had over ten miles of twisting and turning, upping and downing, even before she got to the comparatively straight road across the downs.

Suddenly Jo realised that the Doctor was singing a jolly little song.

She grinned to herself. She could never be cross with him for long. 'You sound happy,' she said. 'You must be very sure this idea of yours will work.'

The Doctor looked surprised. 'I was singing because... oh, because the sky is blue, I suppose.'

'But the Daemon... and the end of the world and all?'

'Oh yes, of course, the end of the world. But that's not now. That would be tomorrow – or this evening – or in five minutes' time. And right now, the sky is blue. Just look at it!'

Jo looked... and looked again. It certainly was blue! A deep, almost cobalt blue overhead fading to a pale greeny duck-egg blue near the horizon.

She stared round, drinking in the blueness, becoming the blueness – and suddenly found that she was singing too!

'See what I mean?' smiled the Doctor.

A taste of *kensho* for Jo?

But this isn't the end of the quest to become awake. Or is it? The very fact that we're on a quest may be the barrier. But what is sure is that this present moment is the gateway through to the other side. And then there's far more than a taste.

PS There's nothing wrong with wine; or women; or song. It all depends on your relationship to them!

In the introduction to this book, I promised that I would hand out a few tips about making films/TV stories, and I've dropped a few hints here and there. But there's one aspect I haven't talked about that is extremely important.

All the time I've been insisting that the story is the most important element.

'Always in the service of the story,' remember?

I went on at length about variety, and about the routine that Terrance and I would follow to help a writer along the way.

Fine. But the danger is that you may come to think that you can construct a viable script like assembling a flatpack wardrobe from IKEA – especially if you've read some of the popular books on scriptwriting (so popular amongst the less creative of producers who, at one stroke, become instant experts and a pain in the butt).

So how should you approach the sometimes daunting task (for it is hard work) of writing a script (or short story, or novel or...)? What is the tip of tips to set you on your way?

Let me remind you about how the brain operates in the world. Recently the neuroscientists have drawn back from the total simplification of the left brain/right brain model; but it is still largely appropriate, and does give us a useful way of discussing the matter.

It has passed into the general consciousness that the left brain operates in a linear, organised way, and deals with language, while the right brain is more holistic, global and intuitive, and is the expert at spatial tasks.

When I was directing studio scenes, I followed the Shaun Sutton method (which was not exclusive to him of course, but which I'd learnt from him) of working out in advance moves for the actors which might arise from the emotional drive of the story, and which would allow for the camera shots which would deliver it to the audience.

After the readthrough, we would then work our way scene by scene, blocking these moves. This was necessary (like the Red Queen in *Through the Looking Glass*, running as fast as possible just to keep in the same place) because of the lack of time.

When we came to the Mad Hatter's tea party in *Alice in Wonderland*, Pip Donaghy, who played the Hatter, objected, being more used to the leisurely ways of the theatre. He wanted to spend time delving into the characters and their interaction by discussion and experiment.

I explained that nothing I'd worked out was non-negotiable, but we had to have a framework. We'd then let the interrelationships grow organically as we worked on the scenes, and if necessary alter the moves and cameras to fit.

Why am I telling you this? It is relevant, I promise you.

When we reached this point, I would sometimes have to create a totally different dance for the cast and cameras from the one I'd choreographed on the kitchen table. To do this, I had to visualise the positions of the various elements, and what would be seen on the screen as a consequence. I'd ask the actors to try the new positions, and I would move around, being each camera in turn and seeing in my mind's eye the resulting shots.

All this without saying a word. I wasn't in the language mode. I was in the right side of my brain, not the left.

And when I came out of this semi-trance, it was quite difficult to get back. I would find myself saying things like, 'I know what's needed. It'll work if, instead of going behind, the March Hare goes in front of the… the… that thing you sit on.'

I couldn't think of the word 'chair'. I was still partly in the right hemisphere.

Incidentally Pip was quite happy in the end. What developed in rehearsal was a family relationship, with the Hatter as Dad, the March Hare as Mum, and the Dormouse as their child.

Oh, and this is a *Doctor Who* story after all. Inside the skin of the adorable little dormouse was the adorable Lis Sladen.

So what is this tip I promised?

Writing is a mixed activity, certainly, using both aspects of the brain.

But if you try to be too organised too soon (left brain), the flow of imagination, of memory, of organic life (right brain) dries up. You'll write a text that fulfils all the criteria but, unless you're very experienced, it runs the risk of being formulaic and dull.

Different writers deal with this in different ways. The method I have described as the one we followed on *Who* was almost entirely right-brain in the early stages of 'brainstorming', sliding towards the centre as we came to our scene-by-scene breakdown and the first draft, and becoming almost totally left-brain in the analysis before the final rewrites.

Others – usually novelists – will prefer to write a first draft at speed, totally immersed in a right-brain trance, and then go back and sort out, with the left brain, the possibly chaotic pile of words and ideas that result. John Braine, who wrote *Room at the Top*, was one of these, as was Georges Simenon – although his 'rewriting' was usually confined to removing redundant adjectives and adverbs.

The ideal, probably, is to have a synthesis of the two, to be very right-brain and very left-brain at the same time, the whole being greater than the sum of the two. When this happens, it's as exhilirating as catching a breaking wave at the right moment and surfing effortlessly shorewards, in control and out of control simultaneously. Unfortunately, unless you happen to be a William Shakespeare (or a Noel Coward), you just have to hope for the right wave to arrive.

Music. Let me tell you about the music for *Who.*

When I took on *Enemy of the World* as director, I didn't even check to find out if I could have specially composed music. I took it for granted that I would have to find appropriate chunks from the gramophone library, from the vast collection of 78rpm and LP discs, preferably from those catalogued as 'mood music', which were free of copyright so that we didn't have to pay the composer and the musicians. These were snippets of varying length, in every style (yes, and mood), to fit any and all requirements, and given titles to match.

One of them was marked, 'Do not use! *Mastermind* theme!' It was entitled *Approaching Menace*. Very apt.

Having sorted out my bits of Bartok, I happened to be asked to join the playback in Shaun's office of one of the episodes of *The Ice Warriors* as part of my initiation into the mystic rites of being a director on *Who*. I was fascinated by the incidental music, which sounded to me like the famous Structures Sonores group, who produced the strangest and most fascinating sounds from odd-looking instruments made of glass.

I asked Derek Martinus, the director, whether the music was by them, and he replied (obviously not wanting to admit that he'd never heard of them!), 'No, but done in a similar way. It's electronic – by the Radiophonic Workshop.'

It had been composed by Dudley Simpson (who used to answer his phone, 'Sidley Dumpson...') and realised by Brian Hodgson. This was the first time I heard synthesised music – though its precursor, *musique concrète*, had been about for some time.

I've recently had a look at the incredibly complete online article, *A History of the Doctor Who Theme* by Mark Ayres (have a look at it. It's well worth it), and discovered, to my complete surprise, that Verity Lambert originally planned to use Les Structures Sonores for the *Who* theme but dropped the idea when they proved difficult to contact. Their music (from LPs) was used for a couple of Hartnell stories though.

Mark also details the changes to the theme that I later asked for as producer.

I loved the original, as did everybody, but I thought it needed a more positive ending – and Brian produced the Zzzzzzzhhh... which admirably does the job.

More tricky, apparently, was the new sound which Delia Darbyshire (who'd realised – with Brian's help – Ron Grainer's original composition) produced in response to my request for a more dramatic beginning to the end titles.

'And now Doctor, I'm going to kill you...' the villain might say. Perhaps the Master does in one of the stories; I can't remember. I'm quite sure there are several thousand readers of this book (I was always an optimist) who could enlighten me.

'And now Doctor, I'm going to kill you...'

And then the closing music oozed in like slow-flowing honey, and all the drama oozed out.

But with Delia's Electronic Scream...!

Honey? Golly gosh, it's more like biting into a jalapeno pepper by mistake.

In 1972, when we were getting ready to celebrate the tenth season of the programme, I asked Brian if he'd like to have another go at the opening, now that synthesisers had been developed. Having been in on the incredibly complicated and laborious construction of the first version in 1963, he jumped at the chance – but of course he had to ask Delia. She agreed that they should have a go.

I had a few doubts about the result. It seemed more tinkly, and somehow thinner than the organ-like original. But having asked them, I felt a certain duty to accept what they'd given me.

It was put onto the first episodes of *The Three Doctors.* And I was going to let it go out, when someone – it may have been Ronnie – told me how much they hated it.

So I asked around, and I found that it was universally abominated. So I dropped it – though, by mistake, it was dubbed onto a couple of export episodes which were shown in Australia. Don't ask me how. Nothing to do with me.

I said the verdict was universal. It couldn't have been more unanimous. I learnt later that Delia and Brian themselves were as disappointed in it as everybody else, but as I'd asked for it they didn't like to tell me.

It really does pay to be honest.

Ah. Something that didn't quite fit into the *Daemons* chapter.

As I told you, the climax was the church blowing up. Obviously a task for Visual Effects. So we called on Peter Day and, after we'd finished filming, he went out to Aldbourne with a load of explosive, no doubt as gleefully as Michealjohn Harris in his Hertfordshire field, rigged it high in the rafters, retired to the village green…

…and blew the roof off the church.

Well, of course he didn't. But the viewer who wrote to the *Radio Times* enraged at the wanton destruction of such a fine old building must have thought that he had done.

How did he achieve such a perfect illusion?

Front-axial projection, that's how. The same process that Ray Harryhausen used for all his fantasy films, such as *Jason and the Argonauts* (remember the fight with the skeletons?), or *The Golden Voyage of Sinbad*; the same process that John Horton was to use in *Carnival of Monsters* to give us our Drashigs, rearing out of the sea marsh; the same process that enabled Chris Reeve to fly in *Superman*.

Another warning! Those of you who aren't technically minded should skip the next bit. My fellow geeks are welcome.

Front-axial projection. The clue is in the title. A projector is attached to the camera mounting at right-angles to the camera itself.

A half-silvered mirror is positioned at an angle of 45 degrees in front, so that the 'plate' (the still, or the moving film), which is to be the background, is projected down the axis of the camera shot.

The screen onto which the projected image is thrown is covered with millions of minute glass beads, each of which has the same property as the 'cat's eye' in the middle of the road: it reflects a beam of light straight back towards its source. So the camera can see the projected picture, even though it has a very low level projection light.

But when the actors are standing in front of the screen, with full lighting on them, the image projected onto them is swamped, so that it can't be seen – and in consequence they are self-matting, just as in the blue-screen process. If somebody in the foreground has to go behind something in the background a shaped matte, covered with the screen material, is stood in front. All clear?

All clear!

It's a remarkably successful process, largely replaced these days by CGI and other computer shenanigans. It does take a long time to set up, as everything has to be positioned very precisely. John Horton, when he was shooting the Drashigs in their Essex bog, said the schedule should allow for only one shot a day!

What else? Oh, yes…

It was quite early in this second year that Terrance and I, getting ahead of ourselves by now, found ourselves deep in discussion about the opening show of the next season. As always, we were determined to think of something that would guarantee us a splash of publicity and a satisfying number of bums on (or behind) sofas.

One thing we realised. In our enthusiasm for the invention of the Master, we'd quite forgotten our own dictum about the necessity for variety. Let's face it, it was just plain silly of us to make him the real villain in every story of his first season.

But it was still a good idea to have introduced him in the first place; and every year we looked for something that would grab the attention as he had done.

We always managed it too. Think of the later seasons:

- *The Time Warrior*: The Doctor's first visit to the past for yonks; and the introduction of our new companion, Lis Sladen as Sarah Jane Smith.
- *The Three Doctors*: the Bill Hartnell, Patrick Troughton and Jon Pertwee incarnations, each convinced that he was the authentic one.
- *Robot*: Tom Baker as the new Doctor.

So what did we come up with to open our third season?

The Daleks.

Producer after producer had decided against using them – largely because of the law of diminishing returns. Remember what I said about variety, and the deadly consequence of repetition? Strange as it may seem, knowing their iconic status as the Doctor's worst enemy, the Daleks had become a bore.

Their viewing figures went down…

And down…

And down…

But now, after five and a half years, we became aware of a widespread feeling that something was missing.

The murmurs became louder and louder; and when the Managing Director of BBC Television himself said to us, 'Where have the Daleks gone?' we knew we'd found our gimmick.

So let me tell you about how *Day of the Daleks* came to be written, and how Terrance and I found ourselves at Pinewood Studios, cracking open a bottle of champagne with Terry Nation.

It happened like this…

No.

I'll tell you next time.

AFTERWORD

Little did I realise, as I timidly entered the office of Barry Letts at the BBC Television Centre – without my glasses, in the throes of a chest infection that resembled kennel cough, and with only one TV credit (as yet unaired) to my name – that this handsome, mild-mannered gentleman would turn out to be a true visionary. As producer of *Doctor Who,* it would be he who laid the new foundations, and turned an innovative and successful children's television programme into the British institution that it is today.

The first thing I was aware of, when I joined the cast in 1970 as the Doctor's companion Josephine Grant, was the chemistry that he sensed when casting his actors – a vital part of any show. Subsequently I realised his courage and insight in taking risks, as we embraced the bright new world of colour television.

He worked tirelessly, improving special effects, carefully choosing production teams and writers, motivating all those around him to reach their full creative potential, and all the while battling the difficulties of a BBC budget.

Under his helm, *Doctor Who* grew up, both technically and scientifically: expanding its audiences and entering the world of cult, but never forgetting its original and younger audience. An early eco-warrior, he opened the doors to the viewers' awareness of the galloping destruction that we are causing here on Earth, something close to my heart then and now.

Thank you for all those wonderful and inspirational years. Barry Letts, you are a champion and a legend in our lifetime.

Katy Manning
September 2009

POSTSCRIPT

Barry always had a warm respect for the fans of *Doctor Who.*

As Barry's family, we would like to thank everyone for their good wishes on the websites and forums following the news that Barry had died.

We have been very touched that the many messages and tributes show such an appreciation and understanding, both of his work and of the very kind and wise man that Barry was.

The Letts family
October 2009

ACKNOWLEDGMENTS

The publishers would like to thank: Crispin Letts; Katy Manning; Terrance Dicks; Fiona Walker and Lindsey Bender at Berlin Associates; Tony Clarke; and Simon Goodman at BBC *Radio Times* Magazine.